The FOUR ~SEASONS~ *Cookbook*

Marshall Cavendish

Editor: Miranda Spicer
Designer: Trevor Vertigan

Published by Marshall Cavendish Books Limited
58 Old Compton Street
London W1V 5PA

ISBN 0 86307 592 4

Some of this material has previously
appeared in the Marshall Cavendish
partwork *Nice 'n' Easy*.

Printed and bound in Spain
by Artes Graficas, Toledo, SA

D.L. TO: 887-1986

Contents

Introduction

Just as each season is memorable for its distinctive weather, the rhythm of the year is also marked by celebrations, feast days and family gatherings which stay in the mind long after the event. *The Four Seasons Cookbook* can help you enjoy those occasions. It includes all the favourite traditional recipes — and suggests others for each of the seasons, using ingredients which are available at the appropriate time of year.

Spring brings snowdrops, daffodils and blossom on the trees. This is the time to enjoy fresh, green vegetables, new potatoes, jam-topped pancakes for

Shrove Tuesday and mouth-watering chocolate Easter eggs. As the weather gradually becomes warmer, and the days stretch into the evenings, the delights of summer cooking begin. Family and guests need little encouragement to eat outdoors in sunny weather. Meals can be either hot or cold, with colourful salads as crisp and healthy starters or as light, nutritious main courses. Delicious and creamy, home-made ice creams are perfect for desserts, as are the sweet summer soft fruits — strawberries, raspberries, blackcurrants and redcurrants.

As summer fades, the rich colours of autumn cover the countryside, and with the harvest come pears, apples and blackberries. Transform these fruits into pickles, pies or puddings. As winter arrives with frosty, cold days, appetites are tempted by warming soups, casseroles and fireside meals, and there are plenty of ideas for these in the final section. The most festive of occasions is undoubtedly Christmas, traditionally associated with lavish food and drink, and home-made sweetmeats.

Every section of *The Four Seasons Cookbook* has an exciting and varied selection of ideas for meat and vegetable dishes; the spring and summer recipes emphasise the fresh flavour of young vegetables and salads, while for autumn and winter there are plenty of nutritious one-pot meals. The highlight of each section is the seasonal menu that completes it: colourful eggs decorate the table at Easter, and there is an elegant dinner-party menu for entertaining on a midsummer's evening. When Bonfire Night arrives, the fireworks display can be enjoyed all the more by everyone, with an easy-to-prepare buffet supper and hot punch. Finally, celebrate Christmas in truly traditional style with roast turkey and all the trimmings, followed by plum pudding and brandy butter.

All the recipes are illustrated in full colour. For your convenience, each recipe is also accompanied by Cook's Notes which contain useful advice and hints on preparation, timing and serving ideas, as well as a buying guide, to help you select the most suitable ingredients. Let *The Four Seasons Cookbook* inspire you to take advantage of seasonal produce at its very best and enjoy the true goodness of home cooking.

SYMBOLS

 TIME
Timing explained including preparation in advance

 FREEZING
The essential guide to dishes which freeze

 ECONOMY
Tips to make dishes go further, or for inexpensive ingredients

 WATCHPOINT
Look out for special advice on tricky methods

 DID YOU KNOW
Useful background to recipes or ingredients

 PREPARATION
Tips for techniques, often with illustrations

 STORAGE
How to store and for how long

 SERVING IDEAS
Suggestions for good accompaniments

 VARIATIONS
How to ring the changes on the basic dish

 COOK'S TIPS
Background information to help when you need it

 BUYING GUIDE
Guide to selecting suitable ingredients

 PRESSURE COOKING
How to save time with your pressure cooker

5

SPRING

Creamy minted lamb

SERVES 4

4 pieces lamb leg steak, each weighing about 175 g/6 oz, trimmed of excess fat (see Buying guide)
25 g/1 oz butter
6 spring onions, chopped
65 ml/2½ fl oz dry white wine
65 ml/2½ fl oz chicken stock
salt and freshly ground black pepper
225 g/8 oz frozen peas, defrosted (see Cook's tip)
2 teaspoons dried mint
150 ml/¼ pint soured cream
mint sprigs or lemon wedges, to garnish

1 Melt the butter in a large, heavy-based frying-pan with a lid. Add the lamb and fry over brisk heat for 2-3 minutes on each side to seal.

2 Add the spring onions to the pan and cook for a further 2-3 minutes, stirring once or twice.

3 Mix together the wine and stock and pour into pan. Season to taste with salt and pepper. Lower heat, cover the pan and simmer for about 1 hour, turning the lamb over occasionally, until it is tender when pierced with a sharp knife.

4 Add the peas to the pan, sprinkle in the mint and stir well. Cook very gently, uncovered, for about 10 minutes or until the peas are tender.

5 Meanwhile, beat the soured cream with a fork until smooth.

6 Remove the pan from the heat and add the soured cream, stirring well to mix. Return to the heat and reheat very gently without boiling. Taste and adjust the seasoning if necessary.

7 Transfer to a warmed serving dish, garnish with mint sprigs and serve at once.

Cook's Notes

TIME
Preparation, including pre-browning the meat, takes about 10 minutes. Cooking takes 1¼ hours.

BUYING GUIDE
Leg steak, available from large supermarkets, is a particularly lean and tender cut of lamb. Although fairly expensive, there is usually very little waste.

COOK'S TIP
It is best to defrost the peas before adding them to the pan otherwise they will tend to make the pan juices too runny.

SERVING IDEAS
Serve the Creamy minted lamb with plenty of plain boiled white rice. For a heartier meal, serve with canned potatoes and baby carrots and, if liked, a tossed mixed salad.

● 430 calories/1800 kj per portion

7 Cut a piece of foil nearly large enough to enclose the lamb. Line a roasting tin with the foil, then put the lamb, skin side up, in the tin. Season with salt and pepper and dust with flour. Pour the oil evenly over the surface of the lamb.

8 Bring the foil up closely around the sides of the lamb but do not cover the surface.

9 Roast the lamb in the oven for 2 hours, basting occasionally with the juices in the foil.

10 Increase oven heat to 200C/400F/Gas 6, open out foil and cook for a further 30 minutes until the skin is crisp and browned and the meat is cooked through (the juices run clear when the lamb is pierced with a fine meat skewer).

11 Remove skewer and transfer lamb to a warmed carving dish. Return to oven turned to lowest setting for 10-15 minutes for meat to 'settle' so that it is easier to carve, then slice and serve.

Spinach-stuffed lamb

SERVES 8

1.5 kg/3-3½ lb shoulder of lamb, blade bone removed (see Buying guide)
plain flour, for dusting
3 tablespoons vegetable oil

SPINACH STUFFING
50 g/2 oz margarine or butter
1 onion, finely chopped
2 celery stalks, finely chopped
225 g/8 oz frozen chopped spinach
250 g/9 oz pork sausagemeat
1 egg, beaten
1 tablespoon finely chopped fresh mint, or 1 teaspoon dried mint
good pinch of freshly grated nutmeg
salt and freshly ground black pepper

1 Make the stuffing: melt the margarine in a saucepan, add the onion and celery and cook gently for about 5 minutes until the vegetables are soft and lightly coloured but not browned.

2 Meanwhile, cook the spinach in a separate pan for about 4 minutes, stirring occasionally. Drain through a fine sieve, pressing with the back of a spoon to remove as much liquid from it as possible.

3 Mix the spinach into the fried onion mixture and cook gently for 1 minute, stirring constantly.

4 Mash the sausagemeat in a bowl. Add spinach mixture and stir well. Stir in the egg, mint and nutmeg. Season well with salt and pepper and mix thoroughly. Cover and refrigerate for 30 minutes.

5 Meanwhile, heat the oven to 170C/325F/Gas 3.

6 With a sharp knife, carefully enlarge pocket left in the lamb by removal of the bone. Pack in prepared stuffing, pressing it down well. Draw edges of pocket together and secure with a meat skewer (see Cook's tip).

Cook's Notes

TIME
Preparing the stuffing takes about 20 minutes, but allow 30 minutes chilling. Preparing the lamb for roasting takes about 15 minutes; cooking 2½ hours; 10-15 minutes for the meat to settle before carving.

BUYING GUIDE
Order the lamb in advance and ask your butcher to remove the blade bone. When stuffed in this way, the shoulder should retain its shape.

COOK'S TIP
If the meat is firmly secured the stuffing should stay in place, but if a little does escape, use it as a garnish for the sliced lamb on the serving dish.

SERVING IDEAS
Serve with roast potatoes and buttered carrots to make an attractive colour contrast with that of the spinach stuffing.

●395 calories/1650 kj per portion

Lamb chops and peppers

SERVES 4

4 large loin lamb chops, trimmed
4 tablespoons vegetable oil
2 medium onions, thinly sliced
1 clove garlic, chopped (optional)
500 g/1 lb tomatoes, skinned,
  deseeded and chopped
2 green peppers, deseeded and cut
  into strips
1 red pepper, deseeded and cut into
  strips
1 teaspoon crushed coriander seeds
  (optional)
salt and freshly ground black pepper
150 ml/¼ pint dry white wine
1 tablespoon tomato purée

1 Heat the oil in a large frying-pan over high heat. Brown the chops on both sides, frying in 2 batches if necessary.
2 With all the chops in the pan, lower the heat, put in onions and garlic, if using, and cover pan. Cook for about 10 minutes until the onions and garlic are soft and beginning to colour.
3 Add the tomatoes, peppers, coriander and salt and pepper to taste. Re-cover the pan and cook for a further 15 minutes or until the chops are tender.
4 Remove chops from pan and keep hot. Raise the heat and stir the wine into the pan. Cook rapidly, uncovered, until the liquid in the pan is reduced by half, stirring constantly.
5 Stir in the tomato purée and simmer, uncovered, for 5 minutes. Taste and adjust seasoning. ✳
6 Place the chops on a warmed serving platter, then spoon the sauce over them. Serve at once.

Country lamb casserole

SERVES 4

1 kg/2 lb middle neck of lamb, cut
    into ribs
1 tablespoon vegetable oil
1 tablespoon dark soft brown sugar
1 tablespoon plain flour
salt and freshly ground black pepper
500 g/1 lb leeks, sliced into rings
425 ml/¾ pint beef stock
400 g/14 oz can tomatoes
250 g/9 oz carrots, cut into chunks
1 bay leaf
1 teaspoon lamb seasoning (see
    Buying guide), or ½ teaspoon
    dried rosemary
1 clove garlic, crushed (optional)
225 g/8 oz frozen runner beans

1 Heat the oven to 230C/450F/Gas 8.
2 Heat the oil in a flameproof
casserole, add the lamb and brown
quickly on all sides. Sprinkle the
brown sugar over the lamb, turning
it until coated. Sprinkle over the
flour and salt and pepper to taste,
then continue frying for a further 5
minutes, turning meat constantly.
3 Transfer the casserole to the oven
and cook for 5 minutes until the
coating on the lamb has caramelized. Remove the lamb from the
casserole and set aside.
4 Lower oven to 170C/325F/Gas 3.
5 Add the leeks to the oil remaining
in the casserole, fry gently on top of
the cooker until soft, then add the
stock and bring to the boil, scraping
up all the sediment from the sides
and bottom of the pan with a
wooden spoon.
6 Return the lamb to the casserole
and add the tomatoes, carrots, bay
leaf, lamb seasoning and garlic, if
using. Simmer, uncovered, for 5
minutes.
7 Cover the casserole, transfer to
the oven and bake for 2 hours or
until the meat is tender. ✳
8 Meanwhile, cook the beans in
boiling salted water according to
packet instructions. Drain, stir into
the casserole and bake in the oven
for a further 5 minutes.
9 Remove from the oven, discard
the bay leaf and taste and adjust
seasoning. Serve at once, straight
from the casserole.

Welsh lamb pie

SERVES 4

8 small lamb loin chops, trimmed of excess fat
salt and freshly ground black pepper
750 g/1½ lb potatoes
40 g/1½ oz dripping or lard
500 g/1 lb leeks, sliced into rings
1 tablespoon plain flour
2 tablespoons chopped fresh mint (see Cook's tips) or 1½ teaspoons dried mint
1 tablespoon milk
75 g/3 oz Caerphilly cheese, coarsely grated (see Cook's tips)

1 Using a small sharp knife, cut the bone out of the chops. Put the bones into a saucepan, cover with fresh cold water and season with salt and pepper. Bring to the boil, then lower the heat, cover and simmer for 20 minutes. Strain the meat stock and set aside.

2 Bring a pan of salted water to the boil, add the potatoes and bring to the boil again. Lower the heat, cover and simmer gently for about 20 minutes until tender.

3 Meanwhile, heat the oven to 180C/350F/Gas 4.

4 Melt the dripping in a large frying-pan, add the chops and fry over moderate heat for 4 minutes on each side. Remove from the pan and drain the chops very thoroughly on absorbent paper.

5 Add the leeks to the pan, turning to coat in the remaining fat, lower the heat slightly and fry gently for 3 minutes.

6 Mix the flour with the mint.

7 Make layers with the leeks and chops in a 1 L/1¾ pint casserole; sprinkle with the flour and mint, and season with salt and pepper between the layers. Spoon over 4 tablespoons stock from the bones, reserving the rest for another use.

8 Drain the potatoes, mash with the milk and season well with salt and pepper. Spread over the top of the pie. Smooth the surface and sprinkle over the cheese.

9 Bake the pie in the oven for 1 hour until the chops are tender and the potato topping is light golden. Serve at once, straight from the dish.

Cook's Notes

 TIME
Preparation, including boiling the potatoes and pre-browning the chops, takes about 30 minutes. Cooking in the oven then takes about 1 hour.

 COOK'S TIPS
Chopped fresh mint can be successfully frozen: press (without adding liquid) into individual ice cube containers or a rubber ice cube tray (for easy removal of the mint cubes) and freeze until solid. Press out cubes, transfer to a polythene bag, seal, label and return to the freezer for up to 1 year. Individual cubes can then be taken out and added frozen to soups and stews, or used to make mint sauce.

If neither fresh nor dried mint is available, spread the chops with 2 tablespoons mint jelly before layering in the casserole.

Unlike Cheddar, Caerphilly cheese does not melt completely when cooked in the oven, but remains in flakes, giving a nice crusty topping to the pie.

●625 calories/2600 kj per portion

Mushroom and lemon pork

SERVES 4-6

1.25-1.5 kg/2½-3 lb joint loin of pork on the bone, rind scored (see Buying guide)
vegetable oil
salt

SAUCE
50 g/2 oz margarine or butter
100 g/4 oz button mushrooms, thinly sliced
25 g/1 oz plain flour
300 ml/½ pint milk
1 teaspoon chopped fresh parsley
finely grated zest and juice of 1 small lemon
salt and freshly ground black pepper
1-2 teaspoons caster sugar

1 Heat the oven to 190C/375F/Gas 5.

2 Rub the rind of the pork all over with a little oil and sprinkle generously all over with salt, for the crackling.

3 Weigh the pork and calculate the roasting time at 35 minutes per 500 g/ 1 lb plus 30 minutes, then place in a small roasting tin and roast in the oven for the calculated time or until the crackling is crisp and brown and the meat is tender (the juices run clear when the meat is pierced with a fine skewer).

4 Meanwhile, make the sauce: melt half the margarine in a small saucepan, add the mushrooms and fry gently for 4-5 minutes until tender. Transfer the mushrooms with their juice to a bowl and reserve.

5 Melt the remaining margarine in the pan, sprinkle in the flour and stir over low heat for 1-2 minutes until straw-coloured. Remove from the heat and gradually stir in the milk. Stir in the parsley, lemon zest and juice and the fried mushrooms with their juice. Season the mixture well with salt and pepper and add sugar to taste.

6 Return the sauce to the heat, bring to the boil and simmer for about 2 minutes, stirring constantly until it has thickened. Remove the pan from the heat.

7 Drain the pork well over the roasting tin and place on a warmed serving dish. Skim any fat from the juices in the pan, then add 1-2 tablespoons of the juices to the prepared sauce and reheat gently if necessary. Serve the pork carved into slices together with the crackling (see Cook's tip) and the sauce handed separately in a warmed sauceboat.

Cook's Notes

TIME
Preparation takes 5 minutes, cooking 2-2¼ hours, including roasting in the oven and making the sauce.

SERVING IDEAS
Serve with crispy roast potatoes. Add colour to the dish by serving with broccoli spears and matchstick carrots.

COOK'S TIP
Before carving remove the crackling in one piece from the top of the joint. Carve the joint into thin slices and serve a little crackling with each portion.

VARIATIONS
Add chopped chives or thyme to the sauce instead of parsley or add a mixture of all 3 herbs. Use 1 small orange instead of the lemon and omit the sugar. Add a little made mustard to taste.

BUYING GUIDE
Ask your butcher to saw through the backbone for easy carving.

●785 calories/3300 kj per portion

Steak and onion parcels

SERVES 4

750 g/1½ lb lean braising steak, trimmed of excess fat and gristle and cut into 4 equal-sized pieces
4 tablespoons vegetable oil
2 large onions, sliced (see Buying guide)
4 teaspoons horseradish sauce
salt and freshly ground black pepper

1 Heat the oven to 170C/325F/Gas 3.
2 Heat the oil in a frying-pan, add the onions and fry gently for 5 minutes until soft and lightly coloured. Increase heat, add steak to pan and fry quickly, turning, to seal and brown.
3 Cut out 4 pieces of foil, each about 30×20 cm/12×8 inches (see Cook's tip). Put 1 piece of steak on each.
4 Spread the steaks with the horseradish sauce and arrange the onions on top. Season well.
5 Fold the foil round the steaks, sealing the ends well to form parcels. Put them on a baking sheet.
6 Cook in the oven for about 1½ hours, until the meat is very tender when pierced with a sharp knife. Serve at once, on warmed individual dinner plates.

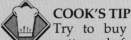
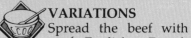

Chicken with watercress stuffing

SERVES 4

1.5 kg/3¼ lb oven-ready chicken
150 ml/¼ pint chicken stock (made from the giblets, if possible)
1 small onion, thinly sliced
bunch of watercress
3 tablespoons chopped parsley
75 g/3 oz fresh wholemeal breadcrumbs
grated zest and juice of ½ medium orange
pinch of ground mace
25 g/1 oz seedless raisins
salt and freshly ground black pepper

SAUCE
300 ml/½ pint chicken stock
grated zest and juice of ½ medium orange

1 Heat the oven to 200C/400F/Gas 6.
2 Put the stock into a saucepan and bring to the boil. Add the onion, cover and cook over low heat for 10 minutes to soften the onion. Uncover, raise the heat and cook until the liquid has reduced by two-thirds. Remove from the heat.
3 Finely chop the watercress and mix it with the onion and stock. Mix in the parsley, breadcrumbs, orange zest and juice, mace, and raisins. Add salt and pepper to taste.
4 Stuff the chicken with the mixture. Tie the legs together and put the chicken on a rack in a roasting tin.
5 Cover the chicken completely with foil, folding the edges of the foil round the rack. Roast for 1 hour. Remove the foil and continue cooking for 20 minutes so the skin becomes brown and crisp. Remove the chicken from the oven and keep it warm.
6 To make the sauce: pour off any fat from the roasting tin, and set the tin on the cooker over moderate heat. Pour in the stock and bring to the boil, stirring in any residue from the bottom of the pan.
7 Add the orange zest and juice and let the sauce simmer while you carve the chicken.
8 Arrange the chicken slices and stuffing on a warmed serving plate. Serve the sauce separately.

Brussels sprouts and Stilton

SERVES 4
250 g/9 oz Brussels sprouts,
  shredded
200 g/7 oz can pimientos, drained
  and sliced
250 g/9 oz Stilton cheese, diced
4 celery stalks, sliced
2 green dessert apples, cored and
  chopped

DRESSING
6 tablespoons vegetable oil
2 tablespoons cider vinegar or white
  wine vinegar
1 teaspoon mustard powder
1 tablespoon snipped chives or
  spring onion tops
salt and freshly ground black pepper

1 Make the dressing: combine the oil, vinegar, mustard and 2 teaspoons of the chives in a screw-top jar. Season with salt and pepper, then shake well to mix.
2 Put the Brussels sprouts in a large bowl. Pour in half the dressing and toss to coat thoroughly. Set aside for 5 minutes.
3 Put the pimientos, cheese, celery and apple into the bowl and toss in the remaining dressing until all the ingredients are thoroughly coated.
4 Serve at once, garnished with the remaining chives.

Cook's Notes

 TIME
Preparation time for this unusual salad is about 30 minutes.

 SERVING IDEAS
Serve as a light lunch or supper dish with slices of crusty French bread.

 VARIATIONS
Shredded raw spinach or any well-flavoured cabbage can be used instead of the sprouts.
  Use other firm blue cheeses such as Danish Blue.

●530 calories/2225 kj per portion

Creamy spring vegetables

SERVES 4
1 small onion, sliced
2 large spring onions, cut into
   1 cm/½ inch slices
2 carrots, cut into 1 cm/½ inch
   slices
50 g/2 oz butter
300 ml/½ pint hot chicken stock
pinch of caster sugar
salt and freshly ground black pepper
250 g/9 oz broad beans (shelled
   weight)
250 g/9 oz peas (shelled weight)
1 teaspoon cornflour
6 tablespoons double cream
1 tablespoon chopped fresh parsley,
   to garnish (optional)

1 Melt the butter in a saucepan, add the sliced onion and spring onions and cook over moderate heat for 2 minutes. Add the sliced carrots and cook for a further 2 minutes, stirring to coat thoroughly.

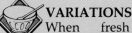

Cook's Notes

TIME
Preparation, if using fresh vegetables, takes 20-25 minutes. Cooking the Creamy spring vegetables takes about 35 minutes.

SERVING IDEAS
This dish is delicious with roast or grilled chicken, pork, lamb or veal. It is also very good as a light lunch or supper dish, simply served with boiled rice, tiny new potatoes or wholewheat rolls.

VARIATIONS
When fresh broad beans and peas are not in season, use frozen ones. Add them to the pan after the carrots have been cooking for 10 minutes, then cook for 8-10 minutes or according to packet instructions.

Add ½-1 teaspoon curry powder to the cornflour when making the sauce to give a mild spiciness to the dish.

●295 calories/1225 kj per portion

2 Pour the hot stock into the pan, add the sugar and salt and pepper to taste, then bring to the boil. Lower the heat, cover and simmer gently for 10 minutes. Add the broad beans and simmer for a further 5 minutes. Add the peas and continue simmering for another 10 minutes, until all the vegetables are tender.
3 Put the cornflour into a small bowl and stir in 1 tablespoon of the hot vegetable stock from the pan. Stir to make a smooth paste, then pour back into the pan. Stir the contents of the pan over low heat for about 4-5 minutes, until the sauce thickens and clears. Stir in the cream and allow just to heat through.
4 Turn the vegetables with the sauce into a warmed serving dish. Sprinkle with parsley, if liked, and serve at once.

Broad beans and peaches

SERVES 4
1 kg/2 lb broad beans (unshelled weight) or 500 g/1 lb frozen
salt
large sprig fresh mint
3 fresh peaches, skinned (see Preparation)
mint sprigs, to garnish

DRESSING
2 tablespoons olive or sunflower oil
1 tablespoon white wine vinegar
2 tablespoons finely chopped fresh parsley or coriander
freshly ground black pepper

1 Bring a large pan of salted water to the boil, add the beans and mint and bring back to the boil. Lower the heat slightly and simmer for about 6 minutes until just tender.
2 Meanwhile, make the dressing:

Cook's Notes

TIME
Preparation and cooking take about 25 minutes, but allow at least 1 hour for cooling.

VARIATION
Use 415 g/14½ oz drained canned peach slices instead of fresh peaches.

PREPARATION
To skin the peaches, immerse in very hot water for 1 minute. Drain, then cut the skin near the stalk and peel away the skin.

SERVING IDEAS
This salad is particularly good with roast lamb, lamb chops or grilled gammon steaks. When serving with hot roast meat, try thickening the dressing with 2 tablespoons yoghurt and adding crushed garlic for extra flavour.

WATCHPOINT
The beans should still be hot when added so that they absorb the flavour of the dressing.

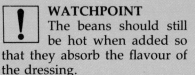

●175 calories/725 kj per portion

pour the oil into a large bowl, add the vinegar, parsley and salt and pepper to taste, then mix well together with a fork.
3 Drain the beans thoroughly, then immediately put them into the bowl of dressing. ☐ Toss well to combine, then cover and leave for at least 1 hour until completely cold.
4 Just before serving, slice the peaches very thinly, then gently stir them into the cold beans. Taste and adjust seasoning, if necessary. Transfer salad to a serving bowl, garnish with mint and serve at once, while peaches are still firm.

Carrots and almonds

SERVES 4

500 g/1 lb carrots, sliced diagonally
  (see Buying guide)
50 g/2 oz flaked almonds, toasted
20 g/¾ oz margarine or butter
20 g/¾ oz plain flour
300 ml/½ pint warm milk
2 teaspoons lemon juice
pinch of ground cloves
salt and freshly ground black pepper
a little finely chopped parsley, to
  garnish

1 Put the sliced carrots into a large saucepan of boiling water, bring back to the boil and boil gently for about 5 minutes, until tender but still firm. Drain well.

2 Heat the grill to high. Toast the almonds on a piece of foil under the grill. Shake the foil occasionally so they brown evenly and do not burn. Remove from the heat.

3 Melt the margarine in a saucepan, sprinkle in the flour and stir over low heat for 2 minutes until straw-coloured. Remove from the heat and gradually stir in the milk. Return to the heat and simmer, stirring, until thick and smooth.

4 Stir in the lemon juice and ground cloves, fold in the carrots and almonds and season to taste with salt and pepper. Heat the mixture through gently, then turn into a warmed serving dish and sprinkle with parsley. Serve at once.

Cook's Notes

TIME
Preparation and cooking take about 45 minutes.

BUYING GUIDE
Choose slender carrots of even thickness through-out their length, so that all the slices are as near the same size as possible.

SERVING IDEAS
Serve with poached fish or grilled pork chops.

●200 calories/850 kj per portion

Stir-fried carrots and peppers

SERVES 4

350 g/12 oz carrots, peeled and cut into 'shavings' (see Preparation)
2 tablespoons vegetable oil
½ onion, finely chopped
½ green pepper, finely chopped
½ red pepper, finely chopped
2 tablespoons soy sauce
2 tablespoons medium sherry
freshly ground black pepper

1 Heat the oil in a wide shallow frying-pan and stir-fry the onion over a moderate heat for 2 minutes. Add the carrots and peppers and stir-fry for about 3 minutes, until carrots are cooked but still crisp.
2 Add the soy sauce and sherry to the pan with pepper to taste. Stir-fry for a further 30 seconds. Turn into a warmed serving dish and serve at once while still piping hot.

Cook's Notes

TIME
Preparing and cooking take 25-30 minutes.

PREPARATION
To make the carrot 'shavings':

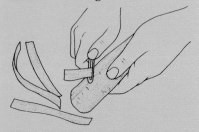

Hold the thin end of the carrot firmly with the fingers of one hand. Rest carrot on board and draw a vegetable peeler along the length of the carrot to make 'shavings'. Turn the carrot, as necessary, to make more shavings.

●100 calories/425 kj per portion

Vegetable medley

SERVES 4
500 g/1 lb spring greens (see Preparation)
salt
25 g/1 oz butter
250 g/9 oz mushrooms, sliced
1 tablespoon lemon juice
6 tablespoons double cream
freshly ground black pepper
350 g/12 oz tomatoes, skinned and sliced
1 teaspoon dried basil
butter, for greasing

1 Heat the oven to 180C/350F/Gas 4 and grease an ovenproof dish with butter.
2 Cook the greens gently for 5 minutes in a small amount of boiling salted water (see Cook's tip).
3 Meanwhile, melt the butter in a saucepan, add the mushrooms and cook over gentle heat until beginning to soften. Add the lemon juice and cook for a further 1-2 minutes. Remove with a slotted spoon.
4 Drain the greens thoroughly in a

colander, squeezing out all the excess moisture by pressing down on the greens with a plate. Transfer to a bowl, stir in the mushrooms and double cream and season to taste with salt and pepper.
5 Put half the greens and mushroom mixture into the greased dish. Cover with half the tomato slices and season with salt and pepper. Sprinkle over half the basil. Turn the

remainder of the greens and mushroom mixture into the dish, smooth the surface and top with the remaining tomato slices. Season again with salt and pepper and sprinkle with the remaining dried basil.
6 Cover the dish with a lid or foil and bake in the oven for 15-20 minutes. Serve at once, straight from the dish.

Cook's Notes

TIME
Preparation, including preliminary cooking, takes 15-20 minutes. Cooking in the oven takes 15-20 minutes.

SERVING IDEAS
This is an unusual and very tasty way of cooking spring greens. To enjoy the flavour fully, serve the dish with simply cooked meat or fish. It is good with liver and bacon.

COOK'S TIP
The secret of cooking greens is to plunge them into a large saucepan containing a small amount of boiling salted water—never drown them in lots of water, because this makes them soggy. Return the water to the boil and boil for the shortest possible time, 5 minutes at the most. Make sure they are drained thoroughly before mixing with the mushrooms and cream.

PREPARATION
To prepare spring greens: cut out the tough central midrib of each leaf and shred the leaves finely.

●175 calories/725 kj per portion

Easter biscuits

MAKES 15

225 g/8 oz plain flour
½ teaspoon ground mixed spice
100 g/4 oz margarine or butter,
  softened
100 g/4 oz caster sugar
grated zest of 1 lemon
1 large egg, beaten
50 g/2 oz currants
1 teaspoon milk
melted margarine or butter, for
  greasing

TO GLAZE
lightly beaten egg white
25 g/1 oz caster sugar

1 Heat the oven to 180C/350F/Gas 4. Brush 2 large baking sheets with melted margarine.
2 Sift the flour with the mixed spice and set aside.
3 Beat the margarine with the caster sugar and lemon zest until light and fluffy. Beat in the egg, a little at a time. Work in the sifted flour, currants and milk, then mix to a stiff dough using a fork.

4 Turn out the dough on to a lightly floured surface and, with a lightly floured rolling pin, roll it out until about 5 mm/¼ inch thick. Cut the dough into rounds with a lightly floured 7.5 cm/3 inch fluted pastry cutter.
5 Transfer the rounds to the prepared baking sheets with a palette knife, then prick each in

several places with a fork. Brush the tops lightly with egg white and sprinkle with caster sugar.
6 Bake the biscuits in the oven for 20 minutes ! or until golden. Let the baked biscuits 'settle' on the baking sheets for 1-2 minutes ! then transfer them to a wire rack. Leave the biscuits to cool completely before serving.

Glazed apple pancakes

MAKES 12
100 g/4 oz plain flour
pinch of salt
1 large egg, lightly beaten
25 g/1 oz butter, melted
300 ml/½ pint milk
butter, for greasing
cream or ice cream, to serve

FILLING AND GLAZE
1 kg/2 lb cooking apples
225 g/8 oz sugar
2 tablespoons water
finely grated zest of 1 lemon
1 rounded tablespoon apricot jam
25 g/1 oz shelled walnuts, chopped

1 Sift flour and salt into a bowl. Make a well in the centre. Add egg, melted butter and 2 tablespoons milk. Whisk together, then slowly whisk in remaining milk.
2 Strain batter into a jug, cover and leave for 30 minutes.

3 Meanwhile, make the filling: peel, core and slice the apples, then put into a saucepan with sugar and water. Cover and cook gently for 15-20 minutes until apples are very soft. Turn into a nylon sieve to drain off excess liquid, then return apples to pan. Stir in lemon zest, cover and keep hot.
4 Heat the oven to 180C/350F/Gas 4.
5 Melt a little butter in a heavy-based 15 cm/6 inch frying-pan over moderate to high heat. Pour off any excess.
6 Whisk the batter. Remove frying-pan from heat and pour in just enough batter to cover base thinly (see Cook's tip). Return to heat and cook pancake for about 1 minute, until underside is set. Using a palette knife, turn pancake over and cook on the other side for 20-30 seconds. Lift pancake on to greaseproof paper.
7 Continue making pancakes, interleaving each with greaseproof paper, until there are 12 altogether. Stir batter frequently and grease pan with more butter as necessary.
8 Spread about 1 tablespoon apple

filling over one-half of each pancake. Fold pancakes in half, then in quarters; arrange in a buttered ovenproof dish and heat through in the oven for 10 minutes.
9 Put jam into a small pan and heat until bubbling. Brush over pancakes, then sprinkle with walnuts. Serve at once, with cream.

Cook's Notes

TIME
Total preparation and cooking time including time for the batter to rest, is about 1 hour.

COOK'S TIPS
As soon as the batter touches the pan, tilt the pan round using a semi-circular action to spread the batter evenly. Use the first pancakes as a 'tester' to judge the amount of batter needed and the temperature of the pan.

●200 calories/830 kj per pancake

Easter Fare

Pretty, colourful eggs, whether to eat or to exchange, and the family gathering for a leisurely weekend meal, are what make Easter such an enjoyable occasion. Attractively marbled boiled eggs will make breakfast a special treat and the festively decorated eggs, which can be made in advance, may be passed round later on. For the main meal, a fruity starter, stuffed lamb and a triumphant meringue-topped pudding will appeal to both young and old.

Marbled eggs

SERVES 6
6 large eggs
2 teaspoons each of green, red and blue food colourings (see Watchpoints)
12 slices white or brown bread, crusts removed
butter, for spreading
2-3 tablespoons sesame seeds

1 Heat the grill to high.
2 Put 2 eggs in each of 3 small saucepans and cover the eggs with water. Add 2 teaspoons of one of the food colourings to each pan and stir well. Bring the water to the boil and boil the eggs for 2 minutes.
3 Meanwhile, toast the bread slices on one side only. Remove from the grill and butter the untoasted sides, then sprinkle generously with sesame seeds. Set aside.
4 Remove the eggs from the water with a slotted spoon and, holding them in an oven glove, gently tap the shells all over with the back of a teaspoon, until they are cracked and crazed. ⚠
5 Return the eggs to their pans, ⚠ bring back to the boil and boil for a further 1-2 minutes for soft eggs or 6-8 minutes for hard-boiled eggs.
6 Meanwhile, toast the sesame-coated sides of the bread until golden brown. Cut the toast into fingers or small triangles.
7 Drain the eggs and rinse under cold running water, then carefully remove the shells. Serve at once, with the sesame seed toast.

Chocolate eggs

MAKES 6
6 large eggs
750 g/1½ lb plain or milk dessert chocolate

DECORATIONS
a little lightly beaten egg white
about 150 g/5 oz icing sugar, sifted
few drops of food colouring (optional)
sugar flowers or other cake decorations

1 Using a small skewer or a large darning needle, very carefully pierce a small hole in both ends of the eggshells. Enlarge one hole in each egg to about 5 mm/¼ inch wide. Hold eggs over a bowl and blow out contents through the larger of the holes.
2 Wash the eggs well in cold water, shaking out any remaining contents and put back in the egg box to drain and dry for about 30 minutes.
3 Meanwhile, make a large and a small piping bag from greaseproof paper, without cutting off the ends.
4 When the eggshells are dry, place a small piece of sticky tape over each of the smaller holes.
5 Put the chocolate in a heatproof bowl over a pan of barely simmering water. Heat gently until melted, stirring occasionally, then pour into the large piping bag.
6 Cut a small hole in the end of the bag and pipe the chocolate into the eggshells. Stand the eggs, sticky tape end downwards, back in the egg box. Allow the chocolate to settle for a few minutes, then top up with a little more chocolate, if necessary. Refrigerate the eggs in the box overnight until set.
7 When the eggs are set, crack them gently, then carefully peel off shells.
8 To decorate: stand each egg in an egg cup. Add a little of the beaten egg white to the sugar and beat until the icing forms stiff peaks, beating in more egg or sugar, if needed. Dot a little icing on to the undersides of the decorations and fix in attractive designs to each egg (see Variations). Add a few drops of food colouring to the remaining icing, if liked, then use to fill the small piping bag. Cut a small hole in the end and pipe leaves or other designs on to eggs.
9 Leave for about 1 hour until set completely. Tie a small ribbon around each egg, fixing with a little icing if necessary.

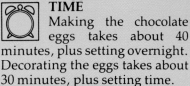
Cook's Notes

Marbled eggs

TIME
Preparing and cooking the eggs and toast take about 20 minutes.

⚠ **WATCHPOINTS**
It is very important to use only edible food colourings to tint the eggs.
Tap the shells very gently to avoid damaging the eggs.
Remember to put the eggs back in the same colour water.

VARIATIONS
Try creating your own designs on the shells of hard-boiled eggs. Use eggs with pale shells and draw or paint on patterns or faces with felt-tip pens, water or oil paints.
The eggs can also be boiled in food colouring to give colour to the shell itself. To create patterns, cut out shapes from masking tape, stick them on to the eggs before boiling in coloured water, then peel the tape away after boiling.

● 400 calories/1675 kj per serving

Chocolate eggs
TIME
Making the chocolate eggs takes about 40 minutes, plus setting overnight. Decorating the eggs takes about 30 minutes, plus setting time.

STORAGE
The decorated eggs can be made up to 1 week in advance, if stored in an airtight container in a cool dry place.

VARIATIONS
Here is a chance for the equipped cake decorator to be really creative. Use 250 g/9 oz icing sugar and 1 large egg white to make the icing. Divide into bowls and add a few drops of food colouring to each. Using a petal nozzle, pipe your own flowers such as pretty daffodils on to non-stick paper, then peel off and fix on to the eggs.

● 755 calories/3175 kj per serving

Melon and orange appetizers

SERVES 6
1 small honeydew melon
3 oranges
1 teaspoon chopped fresh mint, or
  ¼ teaspoon dried mint
2-3 teaspoons caster sugar
6 mint sprigs or matchstick
  strips of blanched orange zest,
  to garnish

1 Cut the melon in half and scoop out the seeds. Cut the flesh into balls with a melon baller and put into a bowl, together with the melon juice (see Variations).
2 Squeeze the juice from half an orange and add to the melon balls. Peel the remaining half orange and the 2 whole oranges over a bowl to catch the juices. Use a fine serrated knife and a sawing action so that the rind is removed together with the pith. Segment the oranges and discard the pips and membranes from between the segments.
3 Add the orange segments and juice to the melon with the mint. Sweeten to taste with caster sugar and mix lightly together.
4 Divide the melon and orange mixture between 6 individual glass dishes and garnish each portion with a sprig of mint.
5 Cover and refrigerate for up to 1 hour before serving.

Lamb with walnut stuffing

SERVES 6
1.5 kg/3-3½ lb leg of lamb,
  boned (see Buying guide)
250 g/9 oz sausagemeat
100 g/4 oz shelled walnuts, finely
  chopped
2 tablespoons chopped fresh
  parsley
¼ teaspoon freshly grated nutmeg
1 teaspoon dried rosemary
salt and freshly ground black pepper
fresh parsley, to garnish

1 Heat the oven to 200C/400F/Gas 6.
2 Put the sausagemeat in a bowl together with the walnuts, parsley, nutmeg and half the rosemary. Season to taste and mix well.
3 Pack the stuffing into the boned cavity of the lamb, then secure with a trussing needle and fine string or meat skewers.
4 Place the lamb, fat side up, on a rack in a roasting tin and sprinkle with the remaining rosemary and salt and pepper to taste. Cover with foil. Roast in the oven for 30 minutes, then lower the heat to 170C/325F/Gas 3 and roast for a further 1½ hours. Remove the foil for the final 30 minutes.
5 Transfer to a serving platter, remove the string or skewers and serve, carved into slices and garnished with parsley.

Cook's Notes

Melon and orange appetizers

 TIME
Preparation time is about 15 minutes, chilling time 1 hour.

 VARIATIONS
Instead of cutting the melon flesh into balls, thickly peel off the skin and cut the melon into cubes.
  Use mandarins or satsumas in place of oranges—use 4 if they are small.
  Add 1 tablespoon toasted almonds for extra crunch.

● 55 calories/225 kj per portion

Lamb with walnut stuffing

 TIME
30 minutes preparation, cooking 2 hours.

 BUYING GUIDE
Ask your butcher to bone the leg of lamb: it is essential to order in advance, especially at Easter time.

 SERVING IDEAS
Serve with a selection of buttered carrots, turnips and new potatoes, and hand round mint jelly.

● 520 calories/2175 kj per portion

Carrots in orange juice

SERVES 4
750 g/1½ lb small carrots, thinly sliced
finely grated zest of ½ orange
juice of 1 orange
25 g/1 oz margarine or butter
1 teaspoon light soft brown sugar
½ teaspoon salt
freshly ground black pepper

TO GARNISH
twist of orange (see Preparation)
sprig of parsley

1 Put the sliced carrots in a saucepan with the orange zest and juice, margarine, sugar, salt and pepper to taste. Add enough cold water just to cover the carrots.
2 Bring to the boil over high heat, then simmer very gently, uncovered, over the lowest possible heat for 40-45 minutes, until the carrots are just tender.

3 Increase the heat and boil the carrots for 4-5 minutes until the amount of cooking liquid has reduced to a few tablespoonfuls. ⚠
4 Transfer the carrots to a warmed serving dish and pour over the remaining cooking liquid. Garnish if desired with a twist of orange, a sprig of parsley and black pepper. Serve at once.

Cook's Notes

 TIME
20 minutes preparation, then 45-50 minutes cooking.

 VARIATION
Use the finely grated zest of 1 lemon and 2 tablespoons lemon juice in place of the orange zest and juice.

 SERVING IDEAS
This dish makes a refreshing accompaniment to any chicken, beef or lamb dish.

 WATCHPOINT
The carrots are boiled for the last 4-5 minutes of cooking to evaporate the water and give the remaining cooking liquid a more concentrated flavour. This is known in cookery terms as 'reduction'. Be careful that you do not reduce the liquid too far, or the little that remains will burn on the bottom of the pan.

 PREPARATION
To make a twist of orange to garnish the carrots, cut a thin slice from the halved orange before you grate it. Cut through the orange slice to the centre, then twist each half in opposite directions. Keep covered with cling film until required.

●100 calories/425 kj per portion

Princess pudding

SERVES 6
25 g/1 oz butter
100 g/4 oz wholemeal breadcrumbs
finely grated zest of ½ lemon
425 ml/¾ pint milk
3 eggs, separated
3 tablespoons black cherry jam
150 g/5 oz light soft brown sugar

1 Heat the oven to 170C/325F/Gas 3. Generously grease a 1 L/1¾ pint ovenproof dish with some of the butter.

2 Mix the breadcrumbs with the lemon zest, milk and egg yolks. Pour into the greased dish and dot with the remaining butter.

3 Bake in the oven for about 40 minutes or until the mixture is set. Remove from oven (see Cook's tip).

4 Put the jam in a small saucepan, heat gently until melted, then drizzle over breadcrumb mixture.

5 In a clean, dry bowl, whisk the egg whites until they stand in stiff peaks. Whisk in the sugar, 1 tablespoon at a time, whisking thoroughly after each addition. Pile on top of the jam and return to the oven for about 20 minutes or until the surface of the meringue is crisp and lightly browned. Serve the pudding at once.

Cook's Notes

TIME
Preparation 20 minutes, cooking 1 hour.

SERVING IDEAS
Serve the pudding with single cream.

COOK'S TIP
For convenience, bake the breadcrumb base before cooking the lamb. When the lamb is cooked, return the pudding to the oven with the jam and meringue topping and cook for just 10 minutes. Turn off oven and finish cooking as the oven cools for 30-40 minutes.

● 280 calories/1175 kj per portion

SUMMER

Lamb ratatouille

SERVES 4

4 large loin or chump lamb chops, trimmed of fat
3 tablespoons olive or corn oil
1 onion, roughly chopped
350 g/12 oz tomatoes, skinned and roughly chopped
1 aubergine, unskinned, cut into 2.5 cm/1 inch cubes
2 courgettes, cut into 2.5 cm/1 inch slices
1 green pepper, deseeded and chopped
1-2 garlic cloves, crushed with ½ teaspoon salt
1 teaspoon dried basil
salt and freshly ground black pepper

1 Heat the oil in a heavy-based deep saucepan, add the onion and fry gently for about 5 minutes until soft and lightly coloured.
2 Stir in the tomatoes, then the aubergine, the courgettes, green pepper, garlic and basil. Bring the mixture to the boil, then lower the heat, cover and simmer for about 30

minutes until the aubergine cubes are soft when pressed with a spoon. Stir the mixture frequently during this time.
3 Heat the grill to high.
4 Uncover the pan of ratatouille, increase the heat and boil rapidly until most of the liquid has evaporated. Taste and season with salt and pepper, then cover the pan again and keep the ratatouille warm on the lowest possible flame, stirring occasionally.
5 Lay the chops on the hot grill rack and grill for about 7 minutes on each side until browned and cooked through.
6 Spoon half the ratatouille into a warmed serving dish, arrange the chops in a single layer on top, then top each with a spoonful of the remaining ratatouille. Serve at once.

Cook's Notes

 TIME
1 hour to prepare and cook the dish.

 DID YOU KNOW
Ratatouille is best described as a French vegetable stew. Native to Provence in the south of France, it is made there with the best of the summer vegetables—aubergines, courgettes, peppers, tomatoes, onions and garlic.

 SERVING IDEAS
Serve with spaghetti, pasta shells or spirals, or boiled or steamed rice.

FREEZING
Ratatouille freezes very successfully, and is a useful vegetable dish to keep in the freezer to serve with any roast or grilled meats. Transfer to a rigid container, cool quickly, then seal, label and store in the freezer for up to 3 months. To serve: reheat from frozen in a heavy-based saucepan, stirring frequently until bubbling. Take care not to overcook the vegetables or they will be mushy. Taste and adjust seasoning before serving.

●750 calories/3125 kj per portion

Cucumber chicken

SERVES 4

4 chicken breasts, each weighing 225 g/8 oz, with skin removed (see Buying guide)
3 tablespoons plain flour
salt and freshly ground black pepper
50 g/2 oz butter
1 tablespoon vegetable oil
1 cucumber, peeled and diced
1 bunch spring onions, finely chopped (see Cook's tips)
300 ml/½ pint soured cream
2 tablespoons chopped fresh mint or 2 teaspoons dried mint
finely chopped spring onion tops, to garnish

1 Season the flour with salt and pepper and put it on a plate. Coat the chicken breasts thoroughly and evenly all over with the flour.

2 Heat half the butter with the oil in a large frying-pan over moderate to high heat. Add the chicken breasts and brown them on both sides. Turn down the heat to low and cook the chicken for about 20-25 minutes, turning occasionally, until the juices run clear when the chicken is pierced in the thickest part with a sharp knife or fine skewer.

3 Meanwhile, bring a saucepan of salted water to the boil, add the diced cucumber and boil gently for 7 minutes. Drain very thoroughly.

4 Melt the remaining butter in a saucepan, add the chopped spring onions and fry gently for 5 minutes. Add the drained cucumber to the pan and mix the vegetables together with a wooden spoon. Add the soured cream and mint and heat sauce gently for a few minutes until hot. ! Season to taste with salt and pepper.

5 Drain the cooked chicken breasts on absorbent paper and place on a warmed serving platter. Spoon a little of the cucumber sauce over each chicken breast, to cover partially. Sprinkle with chopped spring onion tops. Serve at once, with the sauce handed separately.

Halibut special

SERVES 4

**4 × 175 g/6 oz halibut steaks,
  skinned (see Buying guide)**
150 ml/¼ pint dry cider
1 tablespoon cornflour
1 tablespoon cold water
fresh thyme, to garnish

TOPPING
25 g/1 oz butter
1 onion, chopped
2 celery stalks, chopped
3 tomatoes, skinned and chopped
100 g/4 oz mushrooms, chopped
**1 teaspoon chopped fresh thyme or
  ½ teaspoon dried thyme**
salt and freshly ground black pepper

1 Heat the oven to 170C/325F/Gas 3.
2 Make the topping: melt the butter in a saucepan. Add the onion and fry gently for 5 minutes until soft and lightly coloured. Add celery, tomatoes and mushrooms and cook for 1 further minute, stirring once or twice. Add the thyme, season well with salt and pepper and set aside.
3 Arrange the halibut steaks in a single layer in a large shallow oven-proof dish. Spoon the vegetable mixture evenly over the halibut and

pour around the cider. Cover the dish with foil and bake in the oven for about 40 minutes, until the halibut is cooked through and flakes easily when pierced with a sharp knife. Transfer the halibut steaks to a warmed serving dish.
4 Pour the cooking liquid into a small saucepan. Blend the cornflour with the water to make a smooth paste and stir into the liquid. Bring to the boil, stirring constantly. Taste and adjust the seasoning if necessary, then pour over the halibut. Garnish with thyme and serve the halibut at once (see Serving ideas).

Cook's Notes

TIME
Preparation takes about 15 minutes, cooking in the oven about 40 minutes.

SERVING IDEAS
Serve simply with minted garden peas and potatoes gratin dauphinois (sliced and baked with cheese).

BUYING GUIDE
Halibut has a delicious delicate flavour, but is a more expensive white fish than cod or haddock, which can be used instead. Some freezer centres sell economy packs of halibut (1.5 kg/3½-4½ lb).

●230 calories/975 kj per portion

Orange mackerel

SERVES 4

2 mackerel, each weighing 500 g/
   1 lb, filleted
pared rind of 1 large orange
   and finely grated zest of 1 large
   orange
2 bay leaves
salt and freshly ground black pepper
1 lettuce, shredded
8 tablespoons thick bottled
   mayonnaise
2 teaspoons wine vinegar
1 tablespoon top of the milk
segments of 1 large orange and
   watercress, to garnish

1 Put the mackerel fillets into a large shallow frying-pan or roasting tin with just enough water to cover them. Add the orange rind and the bay leaves and season to taste with salt and pepper.

2 Bring to the boil, then lower the heat and simmer for 10-15 minutes until cooked through (the flesh of the fish will separate easily when tested with the point of a knife).

3 With a slotted spoon, carefully transfer the fillets to a large plate and leave to cool completely (see Time). Remove the skin of the fillets carefully with a sharp knife.

4 Arrange the shredded lettuce on a serving plate and lay the cold fish fillets on top.

5 In a bowl, mix the orange zest, mayonnaise, vinegar and milk together. Stir until it is thick and creamy. Spoon half over the fish and serve the remainder in a sauceboat. Alternatively, spoon half into a piping bag, fitted with a large plain nozzle, and pipe on to fish.

6 Arrange orange segments and watercress around the fish. Refrigerate for 10 minutes before serving.

Cook's Notes

TIME
30 minutes to prepare and cook, plus 6-8 hours for the fish to cool.

PRESSURE COOKING
Pour 300 ml/½ pint water or fish or vegetable stock into the base of the pressure cooker. Place a greased trivet, rim-side down in the cooker and place the fish on the trivet. Add zest, bay leaves and salt and pepper. Bring to high (H) pressure and cook for 4-5 minutes. Release pressure quickly. Allow the fish to cool, remove the skin and arrange as described. Then make the mayonnaise mixture and finish as described.

●515 calories/2175 kj per portion

Tuna salad

SERVES 4

200 g/7 oz can tuna, drained and
   flaked
1 crisp lettuce (see Buying guide)
75 g/3 oz can pimientos, drained
425 g/15 oz can red kidney beans,
   drained
175 g/6 oz black olives, stoned
1 onion, sliced into rings

DRESSING

3 tablespoons olive oil
1 tablespoon wine vinegar
½ teaspoon mustard powder
pinch of sugar
1 clove garlic, crushed (optional)
salt and freshly ground black pepper

1 Make the dressing: put all the dressing ingredients into a screw-top jar with salt and pepper to taste. Shake thoroughly to mix, then chill in the refrigerator until ready to use.

2 Line the sides of a large salad bowl with the outside leaves of the lettuce, discarding any damaged leaves.

3 Cut the pimientos into strips.

4 Shred the remaining lettuce (see Preparation) and combine it with the flaked tuna, kidney beans, pimiento and olives. Place in the centre of the salad bowl.

5 Place the sliced onion decoratively on top of the prepared tuna salad to garnish.

6 Pour the dressing over the salad, but do not toss it or you will spoil its appearance, then serve at once. ⚠️

Cook's Notes

 TIME
Preparation takes 10 minutes.

 BUYING GUIDE
A small Webb's or an iceberg lettuce is the best kind for this recipe.

 WATCHPOINT
Do not dress the salad until just before serving or it will become soggy.

 VARIATIONS
Use canned butter or white haricot beans instead of the kidney beans. Add sliced hard-boiled egg for extra nourishment and colour.

 SERVING IDEAS
Serve with hot French bread and/or potato salad.

 PREPARATION
To shred lettuce:

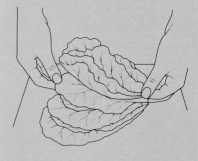

1 *Pile several lettuce leaves on top of each other with the stem ends at right angles to you.*

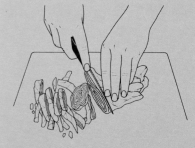

2 *Roll up the leaves, rolling away from you, then slice the roll into thin strips.*

● 305 calories/1275 kj per portion

Chick-pea salad

SERVES 4

100 g/4 oz chick-peas (see Buying
 guide and Cook's tip)
3 tablespoons olive oil
1 tablespoon wine vinegar
salt and freshly ground black pepper
500 g/1 lb tomatoes, skinned and
 sliced
1 medium onion, thinly sliced
2 teaspoons freshly chopped basil,
 or 1 teaspoon dried basil

1 Put the chick-peas into a deep
bowl, cover with plenty of cold
water and leave to soak for 8 hours.
2 Drain the chick-peas, rinse under
cold running water, then put them
into a saucepan and cover with fresh
cold water. Bring to the boil, then
reduce heat and simmer for about 1
hour until tender. Add more water
during cooking if necessary.
3 Drain the cooked chick-peas and
leave to cool.
4 Put the oil and vinegar into a
bowl. Mix together with a fork, and
season to taste with salt and pepper.
Add the chick-peas and mix gently
until well coated with dressing.
Take care not to break them up.
5 Lay the tomato and onion slices in
a shallow serving dish and sprinkle
with the basil and salt and pepper to
taste. Spoon the dressed chick-peas
over the top. Serve cold.

Cook's Notes

 TIME
Preparation takes 15
minutes, plus 8 hours
soaking, then 1 hour cooking for
the chick-peas.

 COOK'S TIP
Preparation time is
greatly reduced by
using a 425 g/15 oz can chick-
peas, well drained and rinsed.

 DID YOU KNOW
Chick-peas are rich in
protein and widely
used in stews and other
traditional dishes in Spain,
India and the Middle East.

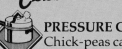 **PRESSURE COOKING**
Chick-peas can be cook-
ed in a pressure cooker.
Soak and rinse as in the recipe,
then cook at high (H) pressure
for 20 minutes.

 SERVING IDEAS
This nourishing salad
can make a complete
light meal, served with soft
wholemeal rolls or warm pitta
bread.
 For a dinner party, serve the
salad as a fairly substantial
starter, provided the main
course is light. It would also be
attractive for a buffet party.

 FREEZING
Chick-peas freeze well
after soaking and cook-
ing. After cooling, freeze in
rigid containers for up to 2
months. Allow several hours for
defrosting at room temperature.

 BUYING GUIDE
With the increased in-
terest in healthy whole-
foods, dried chick-peas are
available from most supermarkets, as well as specialist
health food stores and Asian
food shops.

●195 calories/825 kj per portion

Stir-fried green beans

SERVES 4

500 g/1 lb runner beans, sliced diagonally into 5 cm/2 inch lengths (see Buying guide)
50 g/2 oz margarine or butter
2 back bacon rashers, rinds removed and chopped
1 tablespoon lemon juice (see Cook's tip)
2 tablespoons water
salt and freshly ground black pepper

1 Melt 15 g/½ oz margarine in a large frying-pan, add the bacon and fry uncovered until crisp and lightly browned. Remove the bacon with a slotted spoon, drain on absorbent paper and reserve.

2 Melt the remaining margarine in the pan, then add the lemon juice and water.

3 Add the beans to the pan and stir-fry for about 8 minutes—they should still be fairly crunchy.

4 Stir in the reserved bacon and season with salt and pepper to taste. Stir-fry for 2 minutes to heat through, then tip into a warmed serving dish and serve at once.

Cook's Notes

 TIME
10 minutes preparation, 10 minutes cooking.

 SERVING IDEAS
These beans provide a delicious crunchy contrast to a casserole. They also go well with roast or grilled chicken.

 COOK'S TIP
Half a lemon will give 1 tablespoon juice

 BUYING GUIDE
If fresh beans are not available, frozen beans may be substituted for this dish—do not defrost before using and stir-fry for 3-4 minutes.

● 155 calories/650 kj per portion

Tomatoes with onions and cream

SERVES 4-6

6 large ripe tomatoes (weighing about 500 g/1 lb), halved
3 tablespoons olive oil
500 g/1 lb onions, thinly sliced
salt and freshly ground black pepper
1 tablespoon chopped fresh basil, or 1 teaspoon dried basil
150 ml/¼ pint single or soured cream

1 Cut a cross on the cut sides of the tomato halves (see Cook's tip).
2 Heat the oil in a large frying-pan, add the onions and put the tomatoes, cut side uppermost, on top of the onions. Season well with salt and pepper and sprinkle over the basil.

3 Cook over gentle heat for 7-10 minutes until the tomatoes begin to soften. !
4 Carefully turn the tomatoes over with a fish slice and cook for about 5 minutes on the cut side.

5 Pour the cream over the tomatoes and onions and warm through gently, but do not let the mixture boil. Taking care not to split the tomatoes, transfer to a warmed serving dish and serve at once.

Cook's Notes

TIME
Preparation and cooking take about 20 minutes.

COOK'S TIP
Cutting a cross in the tomatoes helps the heat penetrate evenly and prevents the tomatoes from splitting during cooking.

WATCHPOINT
Do not let the tomatoes overcook or they will become mushy. They should just begin to soften, but still hold their shape. Cooking time will vary according to their ripeness and size.

VARIATION
Try fresh or dried thyme instead of basil.

SERVING IDEAS
This makes a rather special snack if served on fried or hot French bread.

● 210 calories/875 kj per portion

Continental-style cabbage

SERVES 4

**500 g/1 lb green cabbage, cored and
  thinly shredded**
2 tablespoons vegetable oil
2 cloves garlic, crushed
salt and freshly ground black pepper
**2-3 streaky bacon rashers, rinds
  removed**

1 Heat the oil in a large deep frying-
pan over low heat, add the garlic
and cook for 2-3 minutes, stirring
occasionally. Add the cabbage and
season with salt and pepper. [!]
2 Cook for 8-10 minutes or until
tender but still crisp, turning the
cabbage over occasionally so that it
cooks evenly.
3 Meanwhile, heat the grill to high
and grill the bacon for about 2
minutes on each side or until cooked
and crisp. Drain on absorbent paper
and crumble.
4 Transfer the cooked cabbage to a
warmed serving dish and sprinkle
over the bacon. Serve at once.

Cook's Notes

TIME
About 30 minutes pre-
paration and cooking.

WATCHPOINT
Season sparingly as the
bacon will make the
dish salty.

SERVING IDEAS
Cabbage with a differ-
ence, this dish can
accompany many main dishes.
The cabbage is good without the
bacon so can be enjoyed by
vegetarians.

VARIATIONS
You can, of course, use
white cabbage but this
may need a little longer cooking.
Or you can add curry powder
with the garlic and finish with
some fried cashew nuts or
almonds instead of the bacon.

● 110 calories/460 kj per portion

Bean and avocado salad

SERVES 4

225 g/8 oz shelled fresh or frozen
   broad beans (see Buying guide
   and Cook's tips)
salt
1 large avocado
4 tomatoes, thinly sliced

DRESSING

1 tablespoon wine vinegar
2 teaspoons water
1 teaspoon caster sugar
3 tablespoons vegetable oil
good pinch each of freshly ground
   black pepper and mustard powder
1 teaspoon very finely chopped
   onion
1 teaspoon very finely chopped
   mint or ½ teaspoon dried mint

1 Bring a pan of salted water to the boil and cook the fresh broad beans, if using, for 15-20 minutes, until tender. If using frozen beans, cook according to packet instructions. Drain well and leave to cool completely (see Cook's tips).

2 Halve, stone and peel the avocado. Cut the flesh into 1 cm/½ inch dice and put into a bowl with the broad beans.

3 To make the dressing: place all the ingredients in a screw-top jar and shake thoroughly until well blended. Pour over the avocado and broad beans and toss to mix well.

4 Arrange the sliced tomatoes in a border around a serving plate and pile the prepared salad in the centre. Serve at once. ⚠️

Cook's Notes

TIME
Cooking the broad beans takes 15-20 minutes. Allow 30 minutes for cooling. Preparing the salad then takes 10 minutes.

BUYING GUIDE
Yield from beans can vary considerably but 1 kg/2 lb broad beans in the pod should give you enough for this particular recipe.

COOK'S TIPS
Wear rubber gloves when shelling broad beans or they may stain your hands.

When using larger, older beans, remove their skins after cooking and cooling, to leave a bright green, tender bean.

SERVING IDEAS
Serve the salad on individual dishes as a starter or serve as a side salad with grilled meats or fish. If liked, garnish the top of the salad with chopped hard-boiled egg.

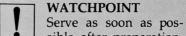

WATCHPOINT
Serve as soon as possible after preparation, or the avocado may start to discolour.

● 285 calories/1200 kj per portion

Courgettes with onion and nuts

SERVES 4
500 g/1 lb courgettes
50 g/2 oz butter
2 tablespoons water
salt
1 onion, sliced into rings
25 g/1 oz pine nuts
freshly ground black pepper

1 Cut the courgettes into quarters lengthways, then cut across to make even-sized sticks.
2 Melt half the butter in a saucepan with the water and a pinch of salt. Add the courgettes, cover the pan and cook gently for 10 minutes until the courgettes are just tender. Shake the pan occasionally during this time to ensure that they cook evenly.
3 Meanwhile, melt the remaining butter in a frying-pan, add the onion rings and fry briskly for 3 minutes until lightly browned. Transfer with a slotted spoon to a plate and set aside.
4 Add the pine nuts to the pan and fry for 2 minutes, stirring, until golden brown.
5 Drain the courgettes, season to taste with salt and pepper, and transfer them to a warmed shallow serving dish. Arrange the onion rings down the centre of the courgettes and sprinkle the pine nuts over the top.

Cook's Notes

 TIME
This easy-to-make vegetable dish takes only 20 minutes to prepare.

 SERVING IDEAS
A tasty way of serving courgettes as a vegetable accompaniment, this dish is excellent with any grilled or roast meat, poultry or fish.

 VARIATION
French or runner beans may be used instead of courgettes very successfully.
Replace the pine nuts with flaked almonds or walnut halves. Alternatively, replace the pine nuts with small cubes of crisply-fried bread.

●105 calories/425 kj per portion

French bean and almond salad

SERVES 4

500 g/1 lb frozen French beans
salt
4 tablespoons olive oil
75 g/3 oz blanched almond halves
(see Buying guide)
juice of ½ lemon
1 tablespoon chopped fresh
parsley
1 teaspoon chopped fresh thyme,
or ½ teaspoon dried thyme
(see Cook's tip)
freshly ground black pepper

1 Heat the oven to 130C/250F/Gas ½. Pour enough water into a large saucepan to come to a depth of 5 cm/2 inches. Add a pinch of salt and bring to the boil. Put in the beans, bring back to the boil and simmer gently for about 10 minutes until just tender. Drain the beans, put

them into an ovenproof serving dish and keep warm in the oven.
2 Heat the oil in a frying-pan, add the almond halves and fry over brisk heat, stirring them around until golden brown on all sides. Remove

the pan from the heat, add the lemon juice, herbs and salt and pepper to taste and stir well.
3 Pour the contents of the pan over the beans and fork through to coat thoroughly. Serve at once.

Cook's Notes

TIME
Preparation, including cooking the beans, takes 30 minutes.

SERVING IDEAS
This salad, which must be served hot, goes perfectly with any roast or grilled meat or poultry and with any fish. It also makes an interesting addition to a variety of salads for a vegetarian meal.

BUYING GUIDE
Almonds are sold both unblanched (with their skins) and blanched. The latter are available whole, halved and flaked or slivered, and can be bought in convenient-sized packets at most supermarkets. For this recipe, buy a 100 g/4 oz packet and use the remainder in cakes or as a decoration for a sweet such as ice cream.

COOK'S TIP
Fresh herbs are really preferable in this salad—they much improve the flavour—so use fresh thyme if you can get it: lemon thyme, if available, would be particularly good.

●245 calories/1025 kj per portion

Gooseberry and orange pie

SERVES 4

150-175 g/5-6 oz shortcrust pastry, defrosted if frozen
little beaten egg or milk and caster sugar, for glazing
cream or custard, to serve

FILLING
750 g/1½ lb gooseberries, topped and tailed if fresh, defrosted if frozen
75 g/3 oz caster sugar
finely grated zest and juice of 1 orange

1 On a lightly floured surface, roll out the pastry to 4 cm/1½ inches larger all round than the top of an 850 ml/1½ pint ovenproof dish.

2 Invert the dish on the rolled-out pastry and cut round the edge with a sharp knife to make a lid. Then cut a strip, the same width as the rim of the dish, from the outer edge of the pastry.
3 Use the trimmings to make decorations, if liked, and refrigerate with the pastry lid and strip.
4 Meanwhile, heat the oven to 200C/400F/Gas 6.
5 Mix gooseberries with caster sugar, orange zest and juice and then spoon into the dish.
6 Dampen the rim of the dish with water. Place pastry strip on rim and press down lightly. Brush pastry strip with egg. Place pastry lid on top of the dish and press round the edge to seal. Trim any surplus pastry, then flute the edge.
7 If using pastry decorations, brush the underside of each one with egg and stick on to the pastry lid. Brush the lid with egg and sprinkle with

caster sugar, then prick with a fork.
8 Bake the pie in the oven for about 30 minutes, until the pastry is crisp and golden. Sprinkle with more caster sugar, if liked, and serve the pie hot with cream or custard.

Cook's Notes

 TIME
20 minutes preparation, plus 30 minutes baking the pie in the oven.

 COOK'S TIP
Use fewer gooseberries but remember that they sink during cooking: a pie funnel can be used to support the pastry lid and prevent it sinking. If you do not have one, use an upturned egg cup.

●305 calories/1275 kj per portion

44

Strawberry and almond gâteau

MAKES 8-10 SLICES
4 large egg whites
250 g/9 oz caster sugar
½ teaspoon vanilla flavouring
1 teaspoon malt vinegar
100 g/4 oz ground almonds
vegetable oil, for greasing

FILLING AND ICING
150 ml/¼ pint whipping cream
3-4 drops vanilla flavouring
250 g/9 oz strawberries
100 g/4 oz icing sugar
1½ teaspoons instant coffee powder
4-5 teaspoons warm water
25 g/1 oz ground almonds, toasted

1 Heat the oven to 180C/350F/Gas 4. Grease two 4 cm/1½ inch deep, 20 cm/8 inch round sandwich tins and line bases with foil or non-stick vegetable parchment paper.
2 In a clean, dry large bowl, whisk egg whites until standing in stiff peaks. Whisk in sugar, 1 tablespoon at a time, then whisk in vanilla and vinegar. Fold in the almonds.
3 Divide mixture equally between prepared tins and level each surface. ⚠ Bake in oven for 15 minutes, then lower heat to 170C/325F/Gas 3 and bake for 25 minutes more.
4 Cool the meringues for 2-3 minutes, then run a palette knife around the sides to loosen and carefully turn out of tins. Peel off the lining paper (see Cook's tips), then leave meringues on a wire rack to cool completely.
5 Make filling: whip cream and vanilla until standing in soft peaks. Put half the cream into a piping bag fitted with a large star nozzle and reserve. Spread remaining cream over 1 meringue. Reserve a few strawberries; hull and slice the rest and arrange over cream. Place remaining meringue on top.
6 Sift icing sugar and coffee powder into a bowl, then stir in enough water to give a coating consistency. Pour icing over gâteau and allow to run down the sides. Sprinkle ground almonds around top edge, then decorate with piped cream and reserved berries (see Cook's tips).

Cook's Notes

TIME
Total preparation time is about 3 hours.

COOK'S TIPS
If the meringues crack slightly, leave so the flat base is uppermost.
Serve the gâteau, at once, while the meringue is still crisp, or refrigerate for up to 3 hours to allow it to soften.

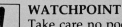
WATCHPOINT
Take care no pockets of air are trapped in the meringue, or it will puff up unevenly during baking.

VARIATION
Use sliced bananas, sprinkled with lemon juice, instead of strawberries.

●340 calories/1425 kj per slice

Chilled chocolate cake

SERVES 8

225 g/8 oz plain dessert chocolate, broken into small pieces
225 g/8 oz unsalted butter
3 tablespoons dark rum
25 g/1 oz caster sugar
2 eggs, separated
150 g/5 oz blanched and ground almonds
12 butter biscuits, broken into small pieces
vegetable oil, for greasing

1 Grease a 1.25 L/2 pint loaf tin.
2 Put the chocolate in a heatproof bowl with half the butter cut into small pieces. Place the bowl over a pan of barely simmering water and heat gently, stirring occasionally, until the chocolate has melted. Stir in the rum, then remove from the heat and leave to cool.
3 In a large bowl, beat the remaining butter with the sugar until light and fluffy. Add the egg yolks, one at a time, beating well after each addition; then stir in the ground almonds.
4 Gradually stir the cooled chocolate into the almond mixture, scraping out the chocolate in the bowl with a spatula (see Cook's tip). Stir until smooth.
5 In a clean, dry bowl, whisk the egg whites until they form soft peaks, then gently fold them into the chocolate mixture with a metal spoon.
6 Gently fold in the biscuit pieces and pour the mixture into the greased loaf tin. Cover tightly with cling film and refrigerate for at least 4 hours until the cake is firm.
7 Unmould the cake 1 hour before serving: run a knife around the sides of the tin, dip the base in very hot water for 1-2 seconds, then invert a chilled serving plate on top of the tin. Hold the tin and plate firmly together and invert them, giving a sharp shake halfway round. Smooth the top and sides of the unmoulded loaf with a palette knife, then return to the refrigerator until ready to serve.
8 Decorate with whipped cream and chocolate (see Serving ideas).

Summer fruit loaf

SERVES 6

500 g/1 lb mixed blackcurrants and redcurrants, stripped from their stalks
225 g/8 oz caster sugar
2 tablespoons water
500 g/1 lb raspberries
6 large thin slices day-old white bread, crusts removed
cream, to serve

1 Put the mixed currants into a heavy-based saucepan with the sugar and water and bring slowly to the boil. Cover and cook gently for 5 minutes, stirring occasionally, until the currants are tender and the juices are flowing.
2 Add the raspberries and cook gently for 2-3 minutes. ⚠ Remove from the heat and strain the fruits, reserving the juices.
3 Use 2 slices of bread to line the base of an 850 ml/1½ pint (500 g/1 lb) loaf tin. Cut bread so that it fits neatly and use the trimmings to fill any gaps. ⚠
4 Spoon half the fruits and 4 table-

spoons of the reserved juices over the bread. Cover with another layer of bread, then spoon in the remaining fruits and 4 more tablespoons fruit juices. Place the remaining white bread on top and press down firmly.
5 Lay a double layer of greaseproof paper on top of the pudding, weight it down and leave in the refrigerator for at least 8 hours (and up to 48 hours). ✳ Refrigerate the

remaining fruit juices separately, in a covered container.
6 To serve: uncover the pudding, then run a round-bladed knife around the sides to loosen it. Carefully turn it out on to a serving dish. Spoon some of the remaining fruit juices over any areas of bread that are not coloured. Serve the summer fruit loaf chilled, with the cream and the remaining fruit juices handed separately.

Ice cream variety

SERVES 6
300 ml/½ pint milk
1 vanilla pod or 2-3 drops vanilla
    flavouring
1 egg
2 egg yolks
75 g/3 oz caster sugar
300 ml/½ pint double cream
crisp biscuits or fan wafers, to
    serve (optional)

1 Pour the milk into a heavy-based saucepan. Add the vanilla pod (see Cook's tips). Bring almost to the boil, then remove from the heat and leave to infuse for 15 minutes. Remove the pod.
2 Whisk the egg with the egg yolks and sugar until pale and creamy, then slowly stir in the vanilla flavoured milk. Strain the mixture into a heatproof bowl.
3 Set the bowl over a pan half full of gently simmering water. ⚠ Cook, stirring constantly, until the custard is thick enough to thinly coat the back of the spoon. Remove the bowl from the pan, cover the custard closely with cling film and leave to cool completely.
4 Whip the cream until just thick enough to retain the impression of the whisk when the beaters are lifted. ⚠ Using a large metal spoon, fold the cream into the custard (see Cook's tips).
5 Pour the mixture into a freezer-proof container. Cover and freeze for 1 hour, or until frozen about 1 cm/½ inch around the sides (see Cook's tips).
6 Turn the mixture into a bowl and whisk thoroughly to break up the ice crystals. Return to the container, cover and freeze for a further 1 hour, then whisk thoroughly again to break up ice crystals.
7 Return to the container, ❄ cover and freeze for 1-2 hours more until mixture is firm.
8 Remove from the freezer and allow to soften for 10 minutes at room temperature before serving. Scoop into individual glass dishes with an ice cream scoop or spoon the ice cream into dishes. Serve with crisp biscuits, if liked.

This luscious ice cream is equally popular with adults and children. It is also extremely versatile and can be flavoured in a variety of ways.

Prepare ice cream up to end of stage 4, then fold in any of following and proceed from stage 5.
Apricot or peach: 400 g/14 oz can apricot or peach halves, drained and puréed with 1 tablespoon apricot or peach brandy added, if liked.
Blackcurrant: 2 × 215 g/7½ oz cans blackcurrants, drained and puréed through a nylon sieve.
Chocolate: 2 tablespoons cocoa powder blended to a paste with 1 tablespoon boiling water and cooled.
Coffee: 2 tablespoons coffee and chicory essence.

Prepare the ice cream to the end of stage 6, then stir in any of following and proceed from stage 7.
Ginger: 50 g/2 oz drained chopped stem ginger and 1 tablespoon of the ginger syrup.

Hazelnut: 100 g/4 oz hazelnuts, toasted, skinned and chopped.
Rum and raisin: 100 g/4 oz seedless raisins soaked in 3 tablespoons dark rum for 1 hour.

Prepare the ice cream up to end of stage 6. Return to container, continue as follows then proceed with the recipe from stage 7.
Ripple: spoon 2 tablespoons sieved raspberries over surface. Swirl through mixture with a skewer: do not overmix or you will lose the ripple effect.

Midsummer Feast

Conjure up your own midsummer night's dream with an elegant dinner-party menu that takes full advantage of all that's fresh and good in summer. Glowing with soft summer colours, our heady meal starts with a delicate asparagus soup and is followed by a sumptuous vision of cucumbered salmon. Sorbet and frosted fruit provide a fantasy finish.

Chilled asparagus soup

SERVES 8
500 g/1 lb fresh asparagus, cut into 5 cm/2 inch lengths (see Buying guide)

1 chicken stock cube
salt and freshly ground white pepper
125 ml/4 fl oz single cream
juice of 2 limes

TO GARNISH
8 whole unpeeled prawns
8 thin fresh slices of lime, cut through to the centre
about 3 tablespoons single cream

1 Bring a large pan of cold water to the boil, add the asparagus pieces and cook for about 15 minutes until soft. Remove the asparagus with a slotted spoon and put in the goblet of a blender.

2 Rapidly boil the liquid left in the pan for 5 minutes, then measure out 1.25 L/2 pints. Add the stock cube to the measured liquid and stir

until dissolved. Leave the liquid to cool slightly.

3 Add a little of the stock to the asparagus in the blender and blend until smooth.

4 Pour the asparagus purée into a large bowl, gradually stir in the remaining stock and season to taste with salt and pepper.

5 Stir in cream, blend thoroughly, then gradually add the lime juice. Cover the bowl of soup with cling film and refrigerate for 2 hours until well chilled.

6 To serve: pour the soup into 8 chilled individual soup bowls and hook 1 prawn and a lime slice over the side of each bowl. Swirl 1 teaspoon of cream into each bowl of soup, and serve at once.

Salmon with fennel mayonnaise

SERVES 8

1.8 kg/4 lb fresh salmon, cleaned and trimmed with head and tail left on (see Buying guide)
1.5 L/2½ pints water
175 ml/6 fl oz dry white wine
1 small onion, finely sliced
1 lemon slice
2 sprigs fresh fennel
1 parsley sprig
1 bay leaf
6 whole black peppercorns
generous pinch of salt

FENNEL MAYONNAISE
150 ml/¼ pint thick bottled mayonnaise
4 tablespoons chopped fresh fennel
1 teaspoon Pernod (see Did you know)

TO GARNISH
1 slice stuffed olive (optional)
1 large unpeeled cucumber, thinly sliced
8 small lettuce leaves
finely chopped fresh fennel
sprigs fresh fennel

1 Pour the water and wine into a large saucepan, then add the onion, lemon slice, fennel, parsley, bay leaf, peppercorns and salt. Bring to boil, then lower heat and simmer for 30 minutes. Cool then strain.

2 Put the salmon into a fish kettle or a large roasting tin and pour over the strained stock. Bring to boil, then turn to the lowest possible heat, cover and simmer gently for 20 minutes until the fish flakes with a fork. Remove the pan from heat and leave fish, still covered, to cool in the liquid overnight.

3 Make the fennel mayonnaise: put the mayonnaise in a bowl with the fennel and Pernod and mix well together. Cover and refrigerate.

4 When the fish is completely cold, dampen a sheet of greaseproof paper with water. Remove the fish carefully from the cooking liquid with 2 fish slices, then transfer to the dampened greaseproof paper.

5 Using the tip of a round-bladed knife, carefully peel off and discard the skin.

6 Roll the fish gently over and remove the skin from the other side, then gently scrape away any bones along sides of fish. Transfer fish to a long serving platter.

7 Garnish the salmon: place the olive slice over the eye, if liked, then completely cover the side of the fish with cucumber slices (see Preparation). Arrange remaining thin cucumber slices around the edge. Arrange the lettuce along one edge of the salmon, and spoon the fennel mayonnaise into the centre of each leaf. Sprinkle the mayonnaise with chopped fennel, then garnish the edge of the dish with fresh fennel sprigs.

COUNTDOWN
The day before
● Cook the salmon and leave to cool overnight.
● Prepare frosted grapes and rose petals and leave to set overnight.
2¾ hours before
● Make the chilled asparagus soup and refrigerate.
2 hours before
● Make the fennel mayonnaise. Skin the salmon and garnish.
● Frost the strawberries.
Just before the meal
● Pour the soup into individual soup bowls and garnish.
Just before the dessert
● Assemble the frosted fruit and rose petals on a dish.

Cook's Notes

Chilled asparagus soup

 TIME
35 minutes to make, plus 2 hours chilling.

! WATCHPOINT
The stock cube will add a certain amount of salt to the liquid so be careful when seasoning.

BUYING GUIDE
Buy the thin green asparagus for this soup or, if available, the kind sold as *sprue* — very thin stalks not regarded good enough for eating whole. They are just as delicious for soup — and much less expensive than the graded varieties of asparagus spears.

●55 calories/250 kj per portion

Salmon with fennel mayonnaise

 TIME
1½ hours preparation, including cooking the salmon; then overnight cooling, plus 20 minutes finishing.

 PREPARATION
Start arranging the cucumber slices at the tail end and overlap them so that they resemble fish scales.

BUYING GUIDE
If a small salmon is difficult to obtain or if you are wanting to economize, substitute salmon trout instead — the colour of the fish is the same and the flavour, though less distinct, is also delicious.

? DID YOU KNOW
Pernod is a French aniseed-tasting drink and is available in miniature-sized bottles. When water is added to Pernod, it turns quite white and cloudy.

●450 calories/1875 kj per portion

Tea sorbet

SERVES 8

10½ teaspoons China tea (see
   Buying guide)
150 g/5 oz sugar
600 ml/1 pint boiling water
juice of 2 lemons
4 egg whites

1 Put the tea into a large heatproof
bowl with the sugar. Pour over the
boiling water and stir until the
sugar has dissolved, then cover and
leave to stand for 1 hour.
2 Strain the tea through a very fine
sieve into a jug. Stir in the lemon
juice, then pour into a 1 L/2 pint
metal loaf tin or other freezerproof
container. Cover tightly with foil
and freeze in the freezer (or freezing
compartment of refrigerator turned
to its coldest setting) for 2½ hours,
or until half-frozen and slushy.
3 Remove from the freezer, turn
into a bowl and mash with a fork to
break up the ice crystals, then
whisk briefly until smooth. Return
to container, cover and freeze for a
further 2 hours, or until firm.
4 In a clean, dry bowl, whisk egg
whites until standing in soft peaks.
5 Remove the tea ice from freezer,
turn into a large bowl and break
up with a fork as before, mashing
well. Whisk the ice until smooth,
then slowly whisk in the egg
whites. Return the mixture to the
container, cover and freeze for a
further 4 hours, until firm. ✳
6 To serve: remove from the freezer
and soften at room temperature for
20-30 minutes. Scoop or spoon into
small serving dishes. Serve at once
(see Serving ideas).

Cook's Notes

 TIME
10-15 minutes prepara-
tion, plus 1 hour stand-
ing and about 8½ hours freezing, plus softening time.

BUYING GUIDE
Choose black China tea:
either Lapsang Suchong
or Keemam, both of which are
available from good supermarkets and specialist food shops.
Do not use Indian or other teas:
they are too strong.

✳ **FREEZING**
Seal the container, label
and return to the freez-
er for up to 3 months. Soften
and serve as in stage 6.

 SERVING IDEAS
The subtle, slightly bit-
ter, flavour of this sor-
bet is best complemented with a
sweet fruit such as strawberries
or raspberries. The frosted fruit
and rose petals on p 53 make a
pretty decoration.

● 80 calories/350 kj per portion

Frosted fruit and rose petals

SERVES 8

large pink rose petals (see Watchpoint)
2 egg whites
100 g/4 oz caster sugar
32 green seedless grapes, separated into small bunches
16 whole fresh strawberries, stalks still attached

1 Lightly beat the egg whites in a bowl and spread the caster sugar on to a flat plate.

2 Frost the rose petals: holding each by tweezers, dip first into the egg white, then sprinkle with the sugar, to coat both sides thoroughly. Spread out in a single layer on a plate, and leave to dry overnight.

3 Frost the green grapes: holding each fruit by its stalk, dip first into lightly beaten egg white, then roll in the sugar. Place on a large flat plate, making sure they do not touch each other, and leave to dry overnight.

4 Two hours before serving, repeat process with the strawberries.

5 To serve: pile the strawberries and grapes carefully into a pyramid on a flat dish, then arrange the rose petals on top.

Cook's Notes

TIME
30 minutes for frosting the rose petals and fruit, plus drying time.

! WATCHPOINT
Do not pick rose petals that have been sprayed with chemicals. Use unblemished petals and wash them carefully but gently before frosting. Hold each at base with a pair of tweezers and quickly dip in very cold water, gently pat dry with absorbent paper.

SERVING IDEAS
These sophisticated frosted fruits and petals are delicious served with lemon sorbet or with Tea sorbet (see p 52).

● 65 calories/275 kj per portion

AUTUMN

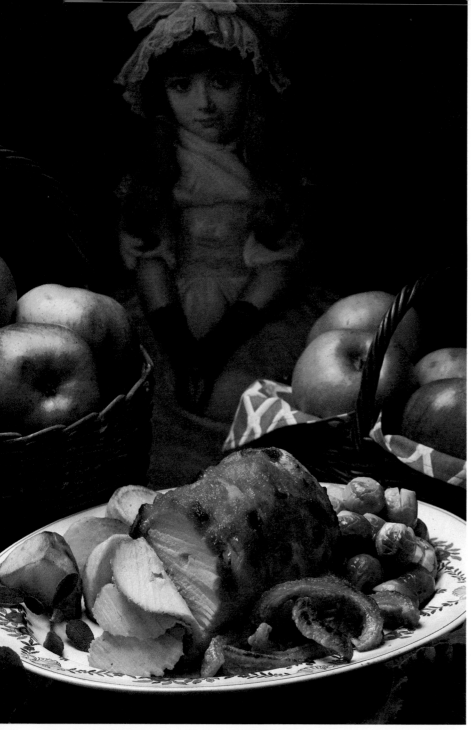

Orchard pork

SERVES 4

1.1-1.4 kg/2½-3 lb loin of pork (see Buying guide)
4 tablespoons dry cider
225 g/8 oz redcurrant jelly
500 g/1 lb cooking apples, peeled, cored and thinly sliced
2 teaspoons dried sage
salt and freshly ground black pepper
vegetable oil, for the crackling

1 Put the cider and redcurrant jelly in a saucepan and heat gently until the jelly begins to melt. Add the apples and cook for 10-15 minutes until soft. Transfer to a blender and work for a few seconds until smooth. Leave to cool.
2 Meanwhile, cut the rind off the pork taking about 5 mm/¼ inch fat with it. Reserve. Weigh pork and calculate cooking time at 30 minutes per 500 g/1 lb, plus 30 minutes.
3 Sprinkle the dried sage over the pork and season with salt and pepper. Put the pork in a deep dish and pour the cool fruit purée over it. Cover loosely with cling film and refrigerate for 3-4 hours.
4 Heat the oven to 200C/400F/Gas 6.
5 Remove the pork from the marinade (do not remove the marinade that is sticking to the fat) and sieve the marinade. Place the pork in a roasting tin and roast in the oven for the calculated time. Cover the pork with foil after 30-45 minutes. [!]
6 Put the pork rind in a baking tin. Sprinkle with salt and brush with oil for the crackling. About 30 minutes before the end of cooking time, place on the highest possible shelf in the oven. Drain off the fat during cooking to ensure crisp crackling.
7 When the pork is cooked (the juices run clear when the meat is pierced with a skewer), transfer to a warmed serving dish with the crackling and keep hot in oven turned to lowest setting.
8 Drain off the fat from the roasting tin, then place the tin on top of the cooker. Stir in the reserved marinade and heat through, stirring constantly. Pour into a warmed sauceboat and hand separately with the pork and crackling.

Cook's Notes

TIME
Preparing the marinade takes 10-15 minutes. Allow at least 3 hours marinating time. Cooking in the oven takes 1¾-2 hours. Making the sauce takes about 5 minutes.

WATCHPOINT
Watch the pork carefully in the early stages of cooking. The marinade mixture can easily burn.

SERVING IDEAS
Serve this roast pork with a difference with roast potatoes and Brussels sprouts or garden peas.

BUYING GUIDE
Ask the butcher to chine the pork but not to bone it, and to score the rind for the crackling.

● 655 calories/2750 kj per portion

Pork loin with Cheddar stuffing

SERVES 4-6

1.25-1.5 kg/2½-3 lb boned loin of
   pork (boned weight), rind scored
   (see Buying guide)
vegetable oil, for brushing
sage leaves, to garnish (optional)

STUFFING

15 g/½ oz butter
1 small onion, chopped
75 g/3 oz Cheddar cheese, grated
75 g/3 oz fresh white breadcrumbs
1 teaspoon mustard powder
1 teaspoon chopped fresh sage or
   ½ teaspoon dried sage
salt and freshly ground black pepper
1 small egg, beaten

Cook's Notes

TIME
Making the stuffing and preparing the pork take 20-25 minutes. Roasting the pork takes about 2 hours.

SERVING IDEAS
Serve with cauliflower florets and courgettes and onions, and a small jug of creamy cheese sauce, if liked.

COOK'S TIP
For crisp crackling, do not baste; raise oven temperature to 220C/425F/Gas 7 for the last 20-25 minutes.

BUYING GUIDE
Ask your butcher to score the rind for you.

●650 calories/2700 kj per portion

1 Heat the oven to 220C/425F/Gas 7.
2 Make the stuffing: melt the butter in a small pan, add the onion and fry gently for about 10 minutes until browned. Remove from the heat and allow to cool slightly.
3 In a bowl, mix together the cheese, breadcrumbs, mustard powder, sage and a generous sprinkling of salt and pepper. Stir in the cooked onion and the egg, mixing well to combine ingredients.

4 Place the pork, fat side down, on a work surface and cut a pocket between the meat and the fat.
5 Spread the stuffing in the cut pocket, then roll up loin, from one long side, and tie at 1 cm/½ inch intervals with fine string. Stand the pork on a trivet in a roasting tin. Brush the rind very lightly with oil, then rub in some salt and freshly ground black pepper.
6 Roast in the oven for 20 minutes, then lower the oven temperature to 190C/375F/Gas 5 and cook for a further 1¾-2 hours (see Cook's tip), until the meat is tender and the juices run clear when the meat is pierced with a skewer.
7 Remove the meat from oven and cut away the string. Allow the meat to cool for 10 minutes, then place on a warmed serving dish and carve into slices. Garnish if liked.

Beef with creamy wine sauce

SERVES 4

1 kg/2 lb rolled topside of beef
40 g/1½ oz lard
350 g/12 oz carrots, sliced
350 g/12 oz leeks, sliced
1 onion, quartered
8 cloves
150 ml/¼ pint red wine
50 ml/2 fl oz water
150 ml/¼ pint soured cream
¼ teaspoon ground mixed spice
salt and freshly ground black pepper

1 Heat the oven to 170C/325F/Gas 3.
2 Melt the lard over moderate heat in a flameproof casserole large enough to take the vegetables and the beef. When the lard is smoking, add the beef and turn to brown on all sides. Remove the beef from the casserole and set aside. Pour away all but 2 tablespoons of the fat in the casserole.
3 Add the carrots and leeks to the casserole and stir, coating the vegetables evenly with the hot fat.

4 Put the browned beef on top of the vegetables. Stick 2 cloves into each onion quarter and arrange them around the beef.
5 Add the red wine and water to the casserole and bring to the boil. Transfer to the oven and cook for 1½ hours, turning the meat once.
6 Remove the beef, discard the string and carve into slices. Remove the vegetables with a slotted spoon and put them on a warmed serving dish. Arrange the sliced beef on top.

Keep hot in lowest possible oven.
7 Boil the cooking liquid in the casserole rapidly for about 5 minutes, until reduced slightly. Remove from the heat and stir in the soured cream and mixed spice. Season to taste with salt and pepper. Heat through very gently, but do not allow to boil. Pour a little of the sauce over the beef, then serve at once, with the remaining sauce handed separately in a warmed sauceboat.

Cook's Notes

 TIME
Preparation takes about 10 minutes. Cooking in the oven, finishing and making the sauce take about 1¾ hours.

 COOK'S TIPS
The sauce is quite thin: if you prefer a thicker sauce, thicken it either with 2 teaspoons cornflour blended with a little water, or with 15 g/½ oz butter mixed to a paste with 1 tablespoon plain flour. Either mixture should be added to the sauce before the cream. Add a little hot sauce to the blended cornflour, then stir into the sauce and let it boil for a minute or two. Whisk in butter and flour paste a little at a time while the sauce is boiling.

 SERVING IDEAS
All that is needed to accompany the meat and vegetables is creamed potatoes, to soak up the sauce.

● 565 calories/2375 kj per portion

Veal and vegetable stew

SERVES 4

750 g/1½ lb pie veal, trimmed and cut into 2.5 cm/1 inch cubes
4 tablespoons plain flour
1 teaspoon garlic salt
freshly ground black pepper
50 g/2 oz margarine or butter
4 carrots, sliced
4 celery stalks, sliced
1 tablespoon sweet paprika
400 g/14 oz can chopped tomatoes
300 ml/½ pint chicken stock
100 g/4 oz button mushrooms
150 ml/¼ pint soured cream

1 Put the veal in a saucepan and pour in enough cold water just to cover. Bring to the boil, then strain. Rinse the scum from the veal under cold running water, then pat the meat dry with absorbent paper.

2 Put the flour, garlic salt and plenty of pepper in a polythene bag. Add the veal cubes and shake until evenly coated. Reserve any excess seasoned flour.

3 Melt the margarine in a large heavy-based saucepan or flameproof casserole, add the veal and fry over brisk heat, stirring until the veal is sealed on all sides. Add the carrots and celery and cook for 2 minutes, stirring. Sprinkle in the paprika and reserved seasoned flour, stir well.

4 Pour in the canned tomatoes with their juice and the stock and bring to the boil, stirring frequently. Lower heat, cover pan and simmer for 40 minutes or until meat is tender.

5 Stir in the mushrooms, cover again and cook for 20 minutes.

6 Remove from the heat, stir in half the cream, then taste and adjust seasoning. Reheat very gently. Do not allow to boil. ! Serve at once, in a warmed casserole if the stew was cooked in a saucepan, with the remaining cream swirled on top.

Port and redcurrant lamb

SERVES 4

16 breakfast lamb chops, defrosted if frozen
salt and freshly ground black pepper
40 g/1½ oz margarine or butter
2 tablespoons vegetable oil
1 red pepper, deseeded and finely sliced
1 tablespoon wholemeal flour
1 tablespoon Worcestershire sauce
300 ml/½ pint chicken stock
4 tablespoons port
4 tablespoons redcurrant jelly (see Economy)
175 g/6 oz small button mushrooms
1 tablespoon chopped fresh parsley

1 Heat the oven to 110C/225F/Gas ¼.
2 Season the chops with salt and pepper. Heat 15 g/½ oz of the margarine with the oil in a large frying-pan. Add the chops and fry over moderate heat for 5-7 minutes,

turning once to brown on both sides. Lower the heat and cook for 2 minutes more on each side. Remove the chops from the pan, arrange them on a warmed serving dish and keep hot in the oven.
3 Add the red pepper to the pan and cook gently for 5 minutes, until softened. Remove the pepper from the pan with a slotted spoon and sprinkle over the lamb chops.
4 Sprinkle the flour into the frying-pan and cook, stirring, for 1-2 minutes. Gradually stir in the Worcestershire sauce, stock, port and redcurrant jelly. Bring to the boil, stirring, then lower the heat and simmer very gently until the redcurrant jelly has melted. Taste and adjust seasoning if necessary.
5 Meanwhile, melt the remaining margarine in a small saucepan. Add the mushrooms and cook gently for about 5 minutes.
6 Strain the hot sauce over the lamb chops and pepper, and arrange the cooked mushrooms around the edge of the dish. Sprinkle with the parsley and serve at once.

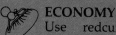

Rum chicken

SERVES 4-6

1.5 kg/3-3½ lb oven-ready chicken
25 g/1 oz margarine or butter
1 tablespoon vegetable oil
100 g/4 oz streaky bacon rashers,
   rinds removed and chopped
250 g/9 oz shallots or small onions
4 tablespoons dark rum
bouquet garni
600 ml/1 pint chicken stock
1 teaspoon soy sauce
1 teaspoon Worcestershire sauce
250 g/9 oz button mushrooms
190 g/6½ oz can pimientos, drained
   and cut into strips (see
   Variations)
salt and freshly ground black pepper

1 Pat the chicken dry with absorbent paper.
2 Heat the margarine and oil in a large flameproof casserole, add the chicken and fry over moderate heat, turning occasionally, until browned all over. Drain well over the casserole and set aside.
3 Put the bacon and shallots in the casserole and fry over moderate heat

Cook's Notes

TIME
Preparation, including pre-cooking, takes about 25 minutes. Cooking takes about 1 hour 10 minutes.

FREEZING
Cut the cooked chicken into portions and arrange in a rigid container. Cover with the sauce and leave to cool completely, then seal, label and freeze for up to 6 months. To serve: reheat either from frozen or defrosted until the sauce is bubbling and the chicken heated through.

VARIATIONS
Omit the strips of pimiento and add 2-3 skinned and chopped tomatoes for the last 5 minutes of cooking time.
   If liked, the sauce may be thickened with a little cornflour.

● 670 calories/2800 kj per portion

for 5 minutes, stirring occasionally.
4 Remove the casserole from the heat and return the chicken to it. Warm the rum over gentle heat in a small saucepan. Remove from the heat, set alight with a match, then pour over the chicken.
5 Add the bouquet garni, stock, soy sauce and Worcestershire sauce to the casserole. Cover and simmer gently for 45 minutes.
6 Add the mushrooms and pimientos and continue cooking for 15-20 minutes or until the chicken is cooked through (the juices run clear when the flesh is pierced in the thickest part with a skewer).
7 Meanwhile, heat the oven to 110C/225F/Gas ¼.
8 Carefully transfer the chicken to a warmed serving dish. Remove the vegetables with a slotted spoon and arrange around the chicken. Keep hot in the oven.
9 Skim the fat from the liquid in the casserole and discard the bouquet garni (see Variations). Taste the sauce and adjust seasoning if necessary. Pour into a warmed sauceboat.
10 Serve the chicken carved into slices; hand sauce separately.

Traditional roast pheasant

SERVES 4-6
2 oven-ready pheasants (see Buying guide)
salt and freshly ground black pepper
75 g/3 oz butter
4 streaky bacon rashers
plain flour, for dredging
watercress and pheasant tail feathers, to garnish

FRIED CRUMBS
50 g/2 oz butter
100 g/4 oz fresh white breadcrumbs

1 Heat the oven to 220C/425F/Gas 7.
2 Wipe the pheasants and remove any remaining feathers. Season them inside and out with salt and pepper and put a 15 g/½ oz knob of butter in each body cavity. Truss and put the birds into a large roasting tin. Lay 2 bacon rashers on each breast and spread the rest of the pheasant flesh with the remaining butter. Pour water into the tin to a depth of 5 mm/¼ inch and roast in the oven for 35 minutes.
3 Remove the pheasants from the oven and discard the bacon rashers. Dredge the breasts with flour. Return to the oven for a further 20 minutes, basting occasionally.
4 Transfer the pheasants to a warmed serving dish, remove the string and keep warm in the oven turned to lowest setting while frying the crumbs.
5 Fry the crumbs: melt the butter in a frying-pan and stir in the breadcrumbs. Fry over moderate heat until golden brown, stirring constantly. Transfer to a small serving dish. Keep warm in oven.
6 Garnish the pheasant with watercress and arrange the tail feathers to complete the dish (see picture). Serve with the fried crumbs (see Serving ideas).

Cook's Notes

 TIME
35 minutes to prepare birds for roasting and frying the crumbs, then 50-60 minutes for cooking.

 BUYING GUIDE
Pheasants are normally sold in pairs (called a brace) and are hung for up to 2 weeks, to bring out the gamey flavour and tenderize the flesh. Look for young birds: this is indicated by soft, even feathers. The long wing feathers should be V-shaped; older birds have round-ended ones. Also look for smooth, pliable legs, short spurs and a firm plump breast.

Ask the butcher or poulterer to pluck and truss the birds, but to leave the feet on.

Frozen pheasants are available from large supermarkets. As with chicken, it is vital to defrost pheasant very thoroughly, to avoid the risk of salmonella poisoning. Defrost frozen pheasant in the refrigerator for 24-36 hours.

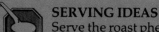 **SERVING IDEAS**
Serve the roast pheasant with bread sauce and game chips (see next page) as well as the crispy fried crumbs. Potato crisps, heated in the oven for 5 minutes, are a good substitute for game chips. Brussels sprouts also go well with pheasant. Make gravy from pan juices, 300 ml/½ pint chicken stock and teaspoon redcurrant jelly.

●410 calories/1725 kj per portion

Game chips

SERVES 4

500 g/1 lb large, even-sized
    potatoes, very thinly sliced (see
    Preparation)
salt
vegetable oil, for deep-frying

1 Put the potato slices into a bowl,
cover with cold water and leave for
30 minutes (change the water every
time it turns cloudy).
2 Drain the potato slices, and pat
dry thoroughly with tea-towels.
3 Heat the oven to 110C/225F/Gas 1/4.
4 Heat the oil in a deep-fat frier
with a basket to 180C/350F or until a
day-old bread cube browns in 60
seconds. Place one-quarter of the
potato slices in the basket, then
lower the basket into the oil and
deep-fry for 2 minutes. Drain on
absorbent paper. Deep-fry the
remaining slices in 3 separate
batches, draining them after frying.
5 Return half the drained potato

 TIME
Preparing the potatoes
takes 5 minutes by
hand, or a few seconds in a food
processor. Frying the potatoes
takes about 20 minutes.

 SERVING IDEAS
As their name implies,
game chips are the tra-
ditional accompaniment to roast
game; they are always served
hot. Try them with pheasant
(see page 62) or, alternatively,
with roast chicken or roast lamb
if you do not usually eat game.

 DID YOU KNOW
Game chips are usually
made using a mandolin,
which is a wooden or metal
hand-operated slicer, fitted
with a straight and a fluted
blade. However, a food
processor fitted with its slicing
blade will do the job just as well.

 PREPARATION
To slice a potato with a
mandolin:

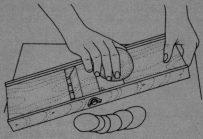

*Rub the potato down over the
straight blade to slice.*

●175 calories/725 kj per portion

slices to the basket, lower into the
oil and deep-fry again for 6 minutes
or until crisp and golden.
6 Drain on absorbent paper and
sprinkle with salt. Transfer to a
serving bowl and keep hot in the
oven while frying the remaining
potato slices in the same way.
7 Pile the second batch of game
chips on top of the first and serve.

Farmhouse lentils

SERVES 4

250 g/9 oz split red lentils
1 tablespoon vegetable oil
1 large onion, thinly sliced
850 ml/1½ pints chicken stock
500 g/1 lb potatoes, cut into even-sized chunks
4 tomatoes, skinned, quartered and deseeded
½ teaspoon dried marjoram or thyme
½ teaspoon sweet paprika
salt and freshly ground black pepper
100 g/4 oz frozen peas
100 g/4 oz button mushrooms, thinly sliced

1 Heat the oil in a large saucepan, add the onion and fry over moderate heat for 3-4 minutes, stirring occasionally.
2 Add the stock to the pan and bring to the boil. Add the lentils, potatoes, tomatoes, herbs, paprika and salt and pepper to taste. Stir well, then cover and simmer for 20 minutes, stirring occasionally. ⚠
3 Add the frozen peas and mushrooms to the pan, cover and simmer for a further 5-10 minutes, stirring occasionally, until the lentils are soft and the potatoes are cooked.
4 To serve: taste and adjust seasoning, then transfer to a warmed shallow dish. Serve hot.

Cook's Notes

TIME
Preparation 10 minutes, cooking 30-45 minutes.

WATCHPOINT
It is important to stir the simmering mixture from time to time, to prevent it sticking to the bottom of the pan as it cooks.

SERVING IDEAS
This dish would go very well with bacon or ham, or plump sausages—especially herb-flavoured ones.

●355 calories/1500 kj per portion

Vegetable stuffed marrow

SERVES 6
1 marrow
250 g/9 oz carrots or swede
2 potatoes
salt
3 tablespoons vegetable oil
15 g/½ oz margarine or butter
1 onion, chopped
4 celery stalks, thinly sliced
50 g/2 oz mushrooms, thinly sliced
1 tablespoon chopped fresh parsley,
   or 1 teaspoon dried parsley
1 egg
150 ml/¼ pint milk
50 g/2 oz fresh white breadcrumbs
50 g/2 oz Cheddar cheese, grated
freshly ground black pepper

1 Cut the ends from the marrow and completely remove the skin if wished. Cut the marrow in half lengthways and, with a tablespoon scoop out and discard the seeds and fibrous tissue (see Cook's tips).
2 Cook the carrots and potatoes together in salted boiling water for 10-15 minutes, until they are almost tender. Drain and leave to cool.

3 Heat the oven to 180C/350F/Gas 4.
4 Heat the oil and margarine in a large frying-pan and fry the onion and celery over moderate heat for 5 minutes, stirring occasionally, until the onion is soft and lightly coloured. Add the mushrooms, stir and cook for 1 minute. Set aside.
5 Cut the carrots and potatoes into 5 mm/¼ inch cubes. Stir them into the frying-pan with the parsley.
6 In a bowl, beat together the egg and milk. Stir in the breadcrumbs and cheese. Pour into the pan, mix and season with salt and pepper.

7 Place the marrow, cut sides up, on a working surface and pack the filling into the cavities of each half. Sandwich the halves of the marrow together again and wrap the marrow closely in foil, sealing the joins tightly.
8 Place the marrow on a baking tray and bake in the oven for 1½-1¾ hours, or until it is tender.
9 Carefully unwrap the foil and, with 2 fish slices, transfer the marrow to a warmed serving dish. Drain off the juices left in the foil into a small sauceboat.

Cook's Notes

 TIME
Preparation and cooking time is 2-2¼ hours.

 COOK'S TIPS
Another way to scoop out the seeds from the marrow is to cut off a slice from each end. Then, using a melon baller or a strong teaspoon, and working from each end, scoop out the seeds and fibres until you have a clear tunnel right through. A tunnelled marrow is easy to slice.

 FREEZING
You can freeze the marrow, ready filled and wrapped in foil, for up to 3 months. To serve: stand the frozen parcel on a baking tray and cook at 190C/375F/Gas 5 for 1¾-2 hours.

 SERVING IDEAS
As the marrow is crammed with vegetables, serve it as a main course.

●240 calories/1000 kj per portion

Pickled cucumber

MAKES ABOUT 1.5 KG/3-3½ LB
2 large cucumbers, total weight about 1 kg/2 lb, scored and thinly sliced (see Preparation)
2 onions, thinly sliced into rings
3 tablespoons salt
600 ml/1 pint white wine vinegar
175 g/6 oz sugar
1 teaspoon mustard seeds
1 teaspoon coriander seeds

1 Layer the cucumbers and onions in a large bowl, sprinkling each layer with salt. Cover and set aside for 2 hours. [!]
2 Meanwhile, select jars with vinegar-proof lids and sterilize them: wash and thoroughly rinse the jars, then stand on a rack or trivet in a large pan of water and bring to the boil. Remove the jars from the pan, stand upside-down to drain, then put in a warm oven to dry out thoroughly.
3 Turn the vegetables out into a colander and rinse well in cold running water to remove the salt. Pat dry on absorbent paper, then spoon the vegetables into the jars, taking care not to pack them in too tightly.
4 Pour vinegar into an enamelled or stainless steel saucepan. Add the sugar and seeds. Bring mixture to the boil, stirring, until the sugar has dissolved, then lower the heat slightly and simmer gently for about 2 minutes.
5 Pour the hot vinegar over the vegetables in the jars, to cover completely, then seal tightly with the vinegar-proof lids. [!] Label and store for at least 2 months before using.

TIME
Preparing and cooking the spiced vinegar mixture take 30 minutes, but allow 2 hours for salting. Store for 2 months before using.

WATCHPOINTS
Do not be tempted to cut the salting process: it is essential to draw out as much water as possible from the cucumber, otherwise the vinegar will be diluted.
Do not use jam pot covers to seal jars. They are not suitable as the vinegar may evaporate, allowing the pickle to shrink and dry out.

PREPARATION
For an attractive finish to the cucumber:

Score along the length of the whole cucumber with a cannelle knife or a fork to remove long thin strips of peel. When sliced, the cucumber will have a fluted edge.

●25 calories/75 kj per 25 g/1 oz

Glazed onions

SERVES 6
750 g/1½ lb small button onions
(see Buying guide)
50 g/2 oz butter
25 g/1 oz sugar
225 ml/8 fl oz chicken stock
1 tablespoon sweet sherry
(optional)
salt and freshly ground black pepper
1 tablespoon chopped fresh parsley,
to garnish

1 Cut off the ends of the onions and remove the skins.
2 Melt the butter in a large frying-pan and add the onions. Cook them over moderate heat, stirring and tossing them frequently, for 10 minutes. Take care that the onions do not burn.

3 Remove from the heat and add the sugar, chicken stock and sherry, if using. Season with salt and pepper to taste. Stir well, return to the heat ✳and continue cooking the onions for 15-20 minutes, until the liquid has evaporated and the sauce is thick and syrupy and the onions are tender. Take special care again at this point, to prevent the onions from burning.
4 Turn the onions into a warmed serving dish and garnish with parsley.

Cook's Notes

TIME
Preparation and cooking time, about 50 minutes.

BUYING GUIDE
You can often buy these small button onions at good greengrocers or supermarkets. As an alternative, you can use shallots but the dish will then have a milder flavour.

FREEZING
To freeze the dish: cook the onions in the stock mixture for only 10 minutes. Cool, transfer to a rigid container, seal, label and freeze for up to 3 months. To serve: defrost at room temperature, continue cooking until the sauce becomes syrupy.

SERVING IDEAS
Glazed onions are a good accompaniment to roast veal, breaded veal escalopes, or roast chicken.

●110 calories/450 kj per portion

Stir-fried celery

SERVES 4

1 head celery, stalks cut into 1 cm/
 ½ inch diagonal slices
1-2 tablespoons vegetable oil
3 spring onions, thinly sliced
salt and freshly ground black pepper
2 tablespoons flaked almonds
2 tablespoons dry sherry
1 teaspoon soy sauce
1 teaspoon tomato purée
½ teaspoon caster sugar
¼ teaspoon ground ginger

1 Heat the oil in a large frying-pan. Add the sliced celery and spring onions and season with salt and pepper. Stir-fry over moderate heat for 5-7 minutes, until the celery has lost its raw taste but is still crunchy (see Cook's tip). Add the flaked almonds and stir-fry for 1 minute.
2 Mix together the remaining ingredients, pour into the pan and stir-fry for 2 minutes. Serve at once.

Cook's Notes

TIME
Preparation takes 15 minutes, cooking 10 minutes.

SERVING IDEAS
Serve stir-fried celery as part of a Chinese meal that you have prepared yourself or bought from a takeaway. It goes well with almost any meat or fish dish, or with a savoury flan or a vegetarian dish such as macaroni cheese.

VARIATIONS
If you do not have any dry sherry, you can use vermouth or white wine instead.

COOK'S TIP
Use a wooden spoon or spatula to stir-fry, keeping the ingredients on the move all the time, so that they cook evenly.

●85 calories/350 kj per portion

Marrow and walnut flan

SERVES 4
1 kg/2 lb marrow, skinned,
    deseeded and roughly chopped
25 g/1 oz shelled walnuts, chopped
215 g/7½ oz frozen shortcrust
    pastry, defrosted
25 g/1 oz margarine or butter
1 large onion, chopped
salt and freshly ground black pepper
50 g/2 oz Cheddar cheese, grated
plain flour, for dusting
walnut halves and tomato slices,
    to garnish

1 Heat the oven to 200C/400F/Gas 6.
2 Roll out the pastry on a lightly floured surface and line a 20 cm/ 8 inch fluted flan dish. Sprinkle half the walnuts over the base of the pastry case and press lightly into the pastry.
3 Prick the base with a fork. Place a large circle of greaseproof paper or foil in the pastry case, weight it down with baking beans and bake blind in the oven for 15 minutes.
4 Meanwhile, melt the margarine in a large frying-pan, add marrow and the chopped onion and fry gently for about 15 minutes until the vegetables are soft. Season to taste with salt and black pepper.
5 Remove the baking beans and greaseproof paper or foil from the flan case and return to the oven for a further 10-15 minutes, until the case is crisp and the sides are beginning to brown.[!]
6 Spoon the vegetables into the cooked flan case and sprinkle the remaining walnuts and the cheese on top. Return to the oven for 5 minutes until the cheese has melted completely.
7 Remove the flan from the oven and allow to cool for 5 minutes. Garnish the flan with walnut halves and tomato slices and serve while warm (see Serving ideas).

Cook's Notes

 TIME
The flan takes about 1 hour to prepare and bake in total.

 SERVING IDEAS
Serve as a vegetarian main meal with baked potatoes and a green vegetable. Alternatively, allow to cool completely and serve cold with a mixed salad.

 VARIATION
Courgettes make a very good alternative to marrow; do not peel them.

! WATCHPOINT
Make sure that the base of the flan case has dried out properly or the flan will be soggy.

●410 calories/1725 kj per portion

Appleberry dumplings

SERVES 6
6 dessert apples
375 g/13 oz can blackberries, drained
juice of ½ lemon
500 g/1 lb frozen puff pastry, defrosted
1 large egg, beaten
caster sugar
cream or custard to serve

1 Heat the oven to 220C/425F/Gas 7.
2 Peel the apples and core carefully with an apple corer or potato peeler. Brush with the lemon juice.
3 Roll out the pastry on a lightly floured surface and trim to 30 x 45 cm/ 12 x 18 inch rectangle, then cut into six squares.
4 Pat the apples dry with absorbent paper. Place an apple on each square of pastry, then divide the drained blackberries equally between the apples, pressing them into the apple cavities.
5 Brush the pastry edges with some of the beaten egg, then wrap each apple loosely but completely, sealing the joins firmly. !
6 Place the dumplings, seam-side down on a dampened baking sheet. Roll out the pastry trimmings and use to make leaves. Brush with cold water and place on top of the dumplings. Brush each one with the remaining egg and sprinkle with caster sugar. ! Make a small hole in the top of each dumpling to allow steam to escape during baking.
7 Bake in the oven for 15 minutes until the apples are tender when pierced with a skewer.
8 Serve with cream or custard.

Cook's Notes

TIME
Preparation and cooking can be completed in 50 minutes.

VARIATIONS
When in season, use fresh blackberries. Also try using blackberry jam or jelly.

WATCHPOINT
While cooking, the apples expand. It is therefore essential to wrap them *loosely* in the pastry or it will break open.
To help prevent the pastry bursting open, make sure the joins are well sealed with egg.

COOK'S TIP
Serve the dumplings straight from the oven. If they are allowed to cool, the apple shrinks back and looks rather sad when you cut through the pastry.

●490 calories/2050 kj per portion

Harvest pudding

SERVES 4-6

225 g/8 oz cooking plums, halved and stoned

500 g/1 lb cooking apples, peeled, cored and sliced

275 g/10 oz sugar

225 g/8 oz fresh or frozen blackberries

8 trifle sponge cakes, cut in half horizontally

softly whipped cream, to serve (optional)

1 Put the plums, apples and 200 g/ 7 oz sugar into a heavy-based saucepan. Cover and cook gently for 10 minutes, stirring occasionally. Add the blackberries and remaining sugar, replace the lid and cook for a further 10 minutes, until all the fruit is very soft.

2 Turn the fruit into a nylon sieve set over a bowl to drain off the excess juice.

3 Arrange a few slices of sponge cake in the base of a 1.5 L/2½ pint pudding basin. Cover the cake with a layer of fruit and sprinkle over about 1 tablespoon of the drained juice. Continue making layers in this way ! until all the cake and fruit are used, finishing with a layer of cake (see Economy).

4 Stand the basin on a plate, then cover the pudding with cling film. Put a small plate or lid which fits just inside the rim of the basin on top of the pudding. Weight the plate down, then leave the pudding in the refrigerator overnight.

5 To serve: run a palette knife around the sides of the pudding to loosen it, then invert a serving plate on top. Hold the plate and basin firmly and invert, giving a sharp shake halfway round. Carefully lift off the basin. Serve the pudding chilled, with cream, if liked.

Iced bramble pots

SERVES 6

250 g/9 oz blackberries (see Buying guide)
2 tablespoons water
50 g/2 oz sugar
3 eggs, separated
75 g/3 oz icing sugar, sifted
¼ teaspoon vanilla flavouring
150 ml/¼ pint double cream

TO SERVE
a few whole blackberries
blackberry leaves (optional)
single cream

1 Put the blackberries into a small pan with the water and sugar. Cover the pan and cook over low heat for about 5 minutes or until the fruit is just tender. Remove from the heat, allow to cool slightly, then pureé in blender or food processor. Work the pureé through a sieve to remove all the pips, then allow to cool completely.

2 Whisk the egg yolks with 25 g/1 oz of the icing sugar until creamy.

3 In a clean, dry bowl, whisk the egg whites until they stand in stiff peaks, then whisk in the remaining icing sugar, 1 teaspoon at a time. Gradually whisk in the egg yolk mixture (see Cook's tips) until the mixture is thick and creamy.

4 Pour one-third of the mixture into a bowl, then stir in the vanilla flavouring. Fold the cold blackberry pureé into the larger quantity of the mixture.

5 Lightly whip the cream until it begins to form soft peaks, then fold one-third into the vanilla mixture and two-thirds into the blackberry mixture.

6 Divide half the blackberry mixture between six 150 ml/¼ pint individual moulds (see Cook's tips and Variation), then spoon the vanilla mixture on top. Spoon the rest of the blackberry mixture on top of the vanilla mixture. Freeze for about 4 hours, until firm.

7 To serve: unmould on to 6 individual plates and decorate with a few blackberries and blackberry leaves, if liked. Serve at once with cream handed separately.

Cook's Notes

TIME
45 minutes preparation, plus cooling time, then 4 hours freezing.

BUYING GUIDE
If fresh blackberries are unavailable, use frozen blackberries, but cook with only 1 tablespoon water.

SERVING IDEAS
Serve with small sweet biscuits or wafers.

●240 calories/1025kj per portion

COOK'S TIPS
It is best to use an electric mixer to whisk the egg yolk mixture into the egg whites, as it is difficult to create enough 'bulk' if whisking by hand.

Small cream, yoghurt or cottage cheese cartons make ideal moulds for this dessert.

VARIATION
This dessert may also be made in one 850 ml/1½ pint mould – a pudding basin or a loaf tin.

Autumn fruit caramel cream

SERVES 6

500 g/1 lb satsumas, divided into
   segments
350 g/12 oz grapes, skinned, halved
   and deseeded
3 bananas
2 tablespoons brandy
300 ml/½ pint double cream
150 g/5 oz dark soft brown sugar

1 Put the satsuma segments into a
1.25 L/2 pint soufflé dish.
2 Add the grapes to the satsumas,
then slice the bananas into the dish.
Stir in the brandy.

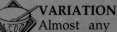

TIME
20 minutes preparation,
plus at least 2 hours
chilling; 2-3 minutes grilling.

COOK'S TIP
The hardened caramel
topping will quickly
soften if the dessert is not
served immediately.

VARIATION
Almost any type and
combination of fresh
fruit can be used in this simple
dinner party dessert. Canned
fruit, as long as it is well
drained, may also be used quite
sucessfully.

●430 calories/1800 kj per portion

3 Whip the cream until it forms soft
peaks, then spoon over the fruit
and gently level the surface with a
palette knife.
4 Cover the dish with cling film and
refrigerate for at least 2 hours.
5 Heat the grill to high.

6 Sprinkle the brown sugar evenly
over the surface of the cream to
cover completely.
7 Place the dish under the hot grill
for 2-3 minutes until the sugar has
caramelized. Serve the caramel
cream at once (see Cook's tip).

Bonfire Party

Bonfire night is sure to be a success with this exciting menu — all the food can be eaten around the fire, so that everyone can enjoy the fireworks to the full. Welcome your guests with a hot wine punch, then serve a selection of hot pasties accompanied by colourful skewers of crispy salad. Finally, offer delicious truffles with cups of steaming coffee.

Hotch-potch pasties

MAKES 24
4 × 400 g/13 oz packets frozen puff pastry, defrosted
little milk, to glaze

FILLINGS
1.25 kg/2½ lb oven-ready chicken
1 small onion
1 carrot, sliced
1 bay leaf
parsley sprig
1 celery stalk, sliced
300 ml/½ pint water
salt and freshly ground black pepper
425-600 ml/¾-1 pint milk
200 g/7 oz can sweetcorn, drained
250 g/9 oz mushrooms, chopped and tossed in juice of 1 small lemon
2 × 200 g/7 oz cans tuna fish, drained
1 tablespoon drained capers
2 tablespoons chopped fresh parsley
25 g/1 oz butter
250 g/9 oz onions, thinly sliced
350 g/12 oz pork sausages, cooked and cooled

SAUCE
75 g/3 oz margarine
75 g/3 oz plain flour
2 chicken stock cubes

1 Wipe chicken inside and out with absorbent paper, place in a large saucepan with the onion, carrot, bay leaf, parsley, celery and water. Season to taste with salt and black pepper. Bring to boil, then lower the heat, cover the saucepan and simmer for about 1 hour, until the chicken is tender.
2 Strain the stock from chicken, discarding the vegetables, then skim the fat from the stock. Make the stock up to 850 ml/1½ pints with the milk and reserve.
3 Cut the chicken flesh into small pieces and put into a bowl with the corn and mushrooms.
4 Put the tuna into a bowl, break up lightly with a fork, then add the capers and parsley.
5 Melt the butter and gently fry the onions; transfer to a bowl. Cut sausages into small cubes and put into a bowl with softened onions.
6 Make sauce: melt margarine in a large pan, sprinkle in flour and stir over low heat for 1-2 minutes. Gradually stir in reserved chicken stock and milk, then add the stock cubes. Simmer, stirring, for about 10 minutes, until thickened.
7 Divide the sauce equally between the bowls of chicken, tuna and sausages. Mix lightly, season to taste with salt and pepper, and leave to cool.
8 Cut six 15 cm/6 inch rounds from each pastry pack. Divide chicken mixture between 12 rounds, tuna mixture between 6 rounds and the sausage mixture between the remaining 6 rounds. Place fillings slightly to one side of each round.
9 Moisten the pastry edges with a little cold water, then fold each pastry round in half to completely enclose the filling. Press edges well to seal and mark with a fork. Make cuts in the top of each pasty, place on baking sheets and refrigerate for 30 minutes.
10 Meanwhile, heat the oven to 220C/425F/Gas 7.
11 Brush each pasty with a little milk, then bake for 25 minutes until golden brown.

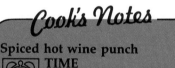

Cook's Notes

Spiced hot wine punch

TIME
30-40 minutes to make the punch in total.

SERVING IDEAS
Although the punch is not boiling hot, it is better to serve it in heatproof glasses with handles.

● 395 calories/1650 kj per glass

Hotch-potch pasties

TIME
About 3 hours to make, 25 minutes baking.

SERVING IDEAS
Serve pasties in napkins with salad on skewers.

● 425 calories/1175 kj per tuna
● 475 calories/2000 kj per sausage
● 375 calories/1500 kj per chicken

Spiced hot wine punch

SERVES 12
2 L/3½ pints red wine
1 lemon
12 cloves
600 ml/1 pint water
500 g/1 lb sugar
thinly pared zest and juice of 2 oranges
thinly pared zest and juice of 1 lemon
2 cinnamon sticks, each 15 cm/ 6 inches long
freshly grated nutmeg
300 ml/½ pint dark rum
150 ml/¼ pint Cointreau
1 orange, thinly sliced, to decorate

1 Cut half the lemon into thin slices, then put the slices on a plate, cover with cling film and reserve. Stud the skin of the remaining lemon half with cloves.

2 Put water into a large saucepan with the sugar, orange zest and lemon zest, clove-studded lemon half, cinnamon sticks and grated nutmeg. Stir until the sugar has dissolved, then bring to the boil. Lower the heat, cover and simmer for 10 minutes. Remove and discard the orange and lemon zest.

3 Add the wine to the pan together with the orange and lemon juice, rum and Cointreau. Heat gently until the punch is very hot – do not allow it to boil. Transfer to bowl.

4 Float the orange slices and the reserved lemon slices on top and serve at once: ladle the spiced hot punch into heatproof glasses (see Serving ideas).

Rum and raisin truffles

MAKES 36

6 tablespoons rum
100 g/4 oz seedless raisins
8 trifle sponge cakes
250 g/9 oz plain dessert chocolate, broken into pieces
75 g/3 oz unsalted butter, diced
100 g/4 oz ground almonds
100 g/4 oz chocolate vermicelli

1 Put the raisins in a small bowl with 3 tablespoons of the rum. Cover the bowl and leave the raisins to soak for 30 minutes.
2 Rub trifle sponges on coarse side of a grater to make crumbs.
3 Put the chocolate pieces in a heatproof bowl with the remaining rum. Place the bowl over a pan of barely simmering water and heat gently, stirring, until the chocolate melts and blends with the rum.
4 Gradually stir the butter into the melted chocolate mixture. Add the sponge cake crumbs, almonds and the soaked raisins and rum. Mix well together, then leave to cool.
5 Sprinkle the chocolate vermicelli on to a baking tray or large plate. Line a tray with cling film.
6 Divide the cooled mixture into 24 walnut-sized pieces, then roll into balls. Roll the balls in the vermicelli (see Preparation), then put on the lined tray. Cover with cling film and refrigerate until firm.
7 To serve: stand 24 petits fours paper cases on a serving platter, then place the truffles in the cases. Refrigerate until serving time.

Bonfire honeycomb toffee

MAKES 36 PIECES
2 teaspoons bicarbonate of soda
225 g/8 oz golden syrup
100 g/4 oz Demerara sugar
25 g/1 oz butter
1 teaspoon malt vinegar
2 tablespoons water
melted butter, for greasing

1 Line a deep 18 cm/7 inch square cake tin with foil, pressing the foil well into the corners.
2 Sift the bicarbonate of soda on to a small plate and reserve.
3 Put the syrup, sugar, butter, vinegar and water into a large, heavy-based saucepan. Clip a sugar thermometer, if using, (see Preparation) to the side of the pan.
4 Bring the mixture slowly to the boil, stirring until the sugar has dissolved and the butter melted. (This takes about 5 minutes.) Then boil steadily, without stirring, for 7-8 minutes, until the thermometer registers 143C/290F (see Preparation).
5 Remove from the heat and stir in the bicarbonate of soda, mixing well. ⚠ Cool slightly. Pour into tin, cool for 15 minutes, then mark into 36 pieces with a sharp knife. Leave to cool completely in the cake tin.
6 Remove the slab of toffee from the tin and peel off the foil. With your hands, snap the toffee into pieces along the marked lines. Serve at once, or store in sealed polythene bags or an airtight container (see Cook's tip).

Cook's Notes

 TIME
Preparation time is about 20 minutes. Cooling takes about 1¼ hours.

⚠ **WATCHPOINT**
Stand well back and use a long-handled wooden spoon as the boiling hot mixture will rise up and froth vigorously for a few seconds.

 COOK'S TIP
To keep the toffees from sticking together, wrap each in cling film or waxed paper. They will keep for several months.

 PREPARATION
To test the temperature without a thermometer:

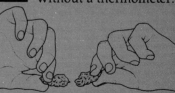

Using a teaspoon, drop some of the mixture into a cup of cold water; leave until solid, then lift out and bend between your fingers: the toffee should snap cleanly and easily. If not, boil for 1 minute more and test again.

●40 calories/160 kj per piece

Winter

Cream of potato soup

SERVES 4
500 g/1 lb old potatoes, diced
50 g/2 oz butter
2 large onions, finely chopped
425 ml/¾ pint milk
425 ml/¾ pint vegetable or chicken
  stock
salt and freshly ground black pepper
4 tablespoons single cream
chopped chives or parsley, to
  garnish

1 Melt the butter in a large pan and, when the foam has subsided, add the potatoes and onions and cook gently for about 5 minutes until the vegetables are soft. Stir frequently to prevent any of the potato dice or chopped onion from sticking to the bottom of the pan.
2 Add the milk and stock (see

Cook's tip), season to taste with salt and pepper and bring to the boil. Lower heat and simmer for 30 minutes, stirring occasionally, until the potatoes are tender.
3 Allow the mixture to cool a little, then work through a sieve or purée in an electric blender.

4 Return the soup to the rinsed-out pan and reheat. Taste and adjust the seasoning, if necessary, and stir in cream just before serving. ⚠ Pour into a large tureen, or ladle into individual soup bowls, garnish with the chopped chives or parsley and serve at once (see Serving ideas).

Cook's Notes

TIME
Preparing and cooking take about 1 hour.

COOK'S TIP
The flavour of this soup is vastly improved by the use of homemade stock, rather than a stock cube.

SERVING IDEAS
This filling soup makes a delicious lunch or supper dish served with slices of hot French bread.

VARIATIONS
Instead of using herbs as a garnish, sprinkle the cream of potato soup with sweet paprika or a chopped hard-boiled egg.

WATCHPOINT
Once the cream has been added to the soup, do not allow it to boil, otherwise the cream will separate and spoil the appearance of the soup.

●305 calories/1275 kj per portion

Chunky soya vegetable soup

SERVES 4

100 g/4 oz soya beans, soaked in cold water overnight (see Watchpoint)
1 tablespoon vegetable oil
50 g/2 oz streaky bacon rashers, rinds removed and chopped
1 large onion, sliced
2 leeks, thickly sliced
50 g/2 oz carrots, thickly sliced
2 celery stalks, thickly sliced
50 g/2 oz turnips, cut into cubes
850 ml/1½ pints chicken stock
1 tablespoon lemon juice
2 tablespoons tomato puree
1-2 teaspoons dried mixed herbs
100 g/4 oz courgettes, thickly sliced
a few tender cabbage or spinach leaves, finely shredded or chopped
salt and freshly ground black pepper
2 teaspoons toasted sesame seeds, to garnish (optional)

1 Drain the soaked beans, then put into a saucepan and cover with fresh cold water. Bring to the boil and boil for 10 minutes, then lower the heat, cover and simmer for 1½ hours.

2 After the beans have been cooking 1 hour 20 minutes, heat the oil in a separate large saucepan. Add the bacon and fry gently for 2-3 minutes, then add the onion and continue cooking for 2 minutes. Add the leeks, carrots, celery and turnips and cook, stirring, for a further 2 minutes.
3 Stir in the chicken stock, lemon juice, tomato puree and herbs.
4 Drain the beans and add to the

pan. Bring to the boil, then lower the heat slightly, cover the pan and simmer for 1 hour.
5 Add the courgettes and cabbage and continue to cook for a further 15 minutes or until the vegetables and beans are tender. Season to taste with salt and pepper.
6 Pour into warmed individual soup bowls and garnish with a sprinkling of sesame seeds, if liked. Serve the soup at once.

Beef and carrot hotpot

SERVES 4

500 g/1 lb beef skirt, trimmed of fat
   and cut into 2.5 cm/1 inch cubes
   (see Buying guide)
250 g/9 oz carrots, thinly sliced
500 g/1 lb potatoes, very thinly
   sliced
250 g/9 oz onions, sliced
2 teaspoons dried mixed herbs
salt and freshly ground black pepper
1 bay leaf
600 ml/1 pint beef stock

1 Heat the oven to 170C/325F/Gas 3.
2 In a deep round casserole
arrange layers of potatoes, carrots,
onions and beef, finishing with a
layer of potatoes. Sprinkle each
layer with herbs and salt and pepper
and add the bay leaf halfway
through building up the layers.

Cook's Notes

 TIME
Preparation takes about
15 minutes, cooking
about 2¼ hours.

 SERVING IDEAS
The hotpot makes an
ideal all-in-one meal,
but if liked, a second vegetable
such as courgettes or cauliflower
may also be served with it.

FREEZING
If the hotpot is to be
frozen, cook it in a foil
container. Cool quickly, cover
and pack in a polythene bag.
Seal, label and freeze for up to 3
months. To serve: unwrap,
cover the foil container with foil
and reheat in a 180C/350F/Gas 4
oven for 1 hour, or until
bubbling all the way through.

 BUYING GUIDE
Skirt is an old
traditional name for the
lean, tender flap of meat inside
the body cavity of the animal at
right angles to the rib cage. It is
often used for braising and is a
good choice for this hotpot as
there is very little wastage and
the flavour is excellent.

●340 calories/1425 kj per portion

3 Pour in the stock, cover the
casserole and cook in the oven for
2 hours.
4 Remove the lid and continue
cooking for 15 minutes until the
potato topping is lightly browned
and all the ingredients are tender
when pierced with a sharp knife.
Serve the hotpot at once, straight
from the casserole.

82

Spiced roast rib of beef

SERVES 4-6

2 kg/4-4½ lb top rib of beef
100 g/4 oz butter
1 clove garlic, crushed (optional)
2 teaspoons English mustard
1 teaspoon ground allspice
1 tablespoon plain flour
watercress sprigs, to garnish

GRAVY

25 g/1 oz plain flour
300 ml/½ pint beef stock
1 tablespoon red wine vinegar or
red wine
salt and freshly ground black pepper

1 Heat the oven to 220C/425F/Gas 7.
2 Weigh the joint and calculate the cooking time, allowing 20 minutes per 500 g/1 lb (see Cook's tip). Place beef on a rack over a roasting tin.

Cook's Notes

TIME
Preparation takes about 10 minutes, cooking takes about 1¾-2 hours.

COOK'S TIP
This cooking time will give a medium rare result. For a well-done roast, add 15 minutes to total time.

SERVING IDEAS
Serve the beef with Yorkshire pudding, roast potatoes, horseradish sauce and a seasonal green vegetable like broccoli. The roast rib joint is equally delicious served cold with salad.

●985 calories/4125 kj per portion

Set aside while making topping.
3 Cream together the butter, garlic, if using, mustard and allspice, then beat in the flour. Spread the mixture evenly all over the meat.
4 Roast the joint for 20 minutes, then lower the oven temperature to 190C/375F/Gas 5, and start the calculated cooking time from then.
5 Transfer the meat to a warmed serving dish and keep warm in the oven turned to its lowest setting.
6 For the gravy: pour off excess fat from the roasting tin, and stir in the flour. Place on top of the cooker, pour in the stock and bring slowly to the boil, stirring constantly and scraping the sediment from the bottom. Add vinegar and simmer for a further 2-3 minutes. Season to taste with salt and pepper, then pour into a warmed gravyboat.
7 Garnish the beef with watercress sprigs and serve at once with the gravy handed separately (see Serving ideas).

Boiled beef and carrots

SERVES 6
1.5 kg/3-3½ lb salted silverside of
   beef (see Buying guide)
1 bay leaf
6 whole black peppercorns
1 onion, quartered
750 g/1½ lb carrots, quartered

PARSLEY SAUCE
25 g/1 oz margarine or butter
25 g/1 oz plain flour
150 ml/¼ pint milk
2 tablespoons finely chopped fresh
   parsley
salt and freshly ground black pepper

1 Put the silverside in a very large saucepan with the bay leaf, peppercorns and onion. Cover with cold water and bring slowly to the boil, skimming off any scum as it rises to the surface. Cover and simmer gently for 1½ hours.

2 Add the carrots to the pan, cover again and simmer for a further 30 minutes, or until the carrots are just cooked and the silverside is tender and flakes slightly when pierced with the point of a sharp knife.

3 Heat the oven to 110C/225F/Gas ¼.

4 Carve the beef and place on a large warmed dish and, with a slotted spoon, arrange the carrots around it. Keep warm in the oven. Blot off surface fat from the pan and reserve the stock for making the parsley sauce.

5 Make the parsley sauce: melt the margarine in a small saucepan. Sprinkle in the flour and stir over low heat for 1-2 minutes until straw-coloured. Remove from the heat and gradually stir in 150 ml/¼ pint of the reserved stock and the milk. Return to the heat and simmer, stirring, until thick and smooth. Stir in three-quarters of the parsley and season to taste with salt and pepper.

6 Remove the boiled beef and the carrots from the oven and serve at once. Hand the sauce separately in a warmed jug. Sprinkle with the remaining parsley before serving.

Cook's Notes

 TIME
Preparation takes 15-20 minutes. Cooking takes about 2½ hours.

 BUYING GUIDE
Salted silverside is available from traditional family butchers and some supermarkets. You may have to order it in advance, in which case allow 2-3 days for the butcher to soak it in brine. The raw salted meat looks rather grey, but turns a rich red when cooked.

DID YOU KNOW
Boiled beef and carrots is a traditional English cold-weather dish. Particularly popular with Londoners, it is celebrated in the Cockney song of the same title.

 SERVING IDEAS
Serve with lightly boiled cabbage and boiled or mashed potatoes, accompanied by English mustard or horseradish sauce.

●430 calories/1800 kj per portion

Farmer's beef

SERVES 4

1 kg/2 lb stewing beef, trimmed of
   excess fat and cut into 2.5 cm/1
   inch cubes
2 tablespoons plain flour
salt and freshly ground black pepper
½ tea_poon dried mixed herbs
25 g/1 oz margarine or butter
1 tablespoon vegetable oil
1 large onion, sliced
700 ml/1¼ pints beef stock
1 bay leaf
500 g/1 lb small potatoes (see
   Buying guide)
100 g/4 oz small button mushrooms
225 g/8 oz shelled fresh peas, or
   frozen peas defrosted

TO GARNISH

2 tablespoons soured cream
1 teaspoon chopped fresh parsley

1 Heat the oven to 170C/325F/Gas 3.
2 Put the flour in a polythene bag,
season with salt and pepper and add
the herbs. Add the beef cubes and
shake until they are evenly coated.
Reserve any excess seasoned flour.
3 Heat the margarine and oil in a
heavy-based frying pan. Add one-
third of the beef cubes and fry over
brisk heat for a few minutes,
turning them to brown evenly.
Using a slotted spoon, transfer the
beef to an ovenproof casserole. Fry
the remaining beef in 2 batches, and
transfer to the casserole.
4 Add the onion to the juices in the
frying-pan and fry gently for 5
minutes until soft. Pour in the stock,
add the bay leaf and bring to the
boil. Pour over the meat in the
casserole. Stir well, cover and cook
in the oven for 1½ hours. ✳
5 Remove the casserole from the
oven, add the potatoes, cover and
return to the oven for a further 45
minutes.
6 Remove the casserole from the
oven, add the mushrooms and peas,
cover again and return to the oven
for 15 minutes until tender.
7 Swirl soured cream over top and
sprinkle with parsley. Serve at once.

Cook's Notes

TIME
Preparation 30 minutes;
cooking 2½ hours.

BUYING GUIDE
Canned potatoes may
be used: cook the cas-
serole for 2¼ hours in stage 4,
omit stage 5 and add the drained
potatoes in stage 6.

FREEZING
Transfer to a rigid
container at the end of
stage 4, cool quickly, then seal,
label and freeze for up to 3
months. To serve: defrost
overnight in the refrigerator or
at room temperature for 4-6
hours, then reheat for 45
minutes in a 180C/350F/Gas 4
oven. Omit stage 5 and proceed
from stage 6, adding 500 g/1 lb
drained canned potatoes or pre-
cooked potatoes.

● 675 calories/2825 kj per portion

Beef and oatmeal stew

SERVES 4

500 g/1 lb lean stewing beef, trimmed of excess fat and cut into 2.5 cm/1 inch cubes
4 tablespoons vegetable oil
2 onions, thinly sliced
3 tablespoons fine oatmeal (see Cook's tip)
salt and freshly ground black pepper
1 teaspoon yeast extract
300 ml/½ pint boiling water
500 g/1 lb frozen mixed vegetables

1 Heat the oven to 170C/325F/Gas 3.
2 Heat half the oil in a frying-pan. Add the onions and fry gently for 5 minutes until soft and lightly coloured. Using a slotted spoon, transfer the onions to a casserole.
3 Put the oatmeal in a polythene bag and season with salt and pepper. Add the beef cubes and shake well to coat the meat thoroughly in the seasoned oatmeal.
4 Heat the remaining oil in the frying-pan, add the coated beef cubes and fry briskly for a few minutes, stirring until sealed and browned. Using a slotted spoon, transfer the browned beef cubes to the casserole.
5 Mix together the yeast extract and water and pour into the frying-pan. Bring to the boil, stirring constantly with a wooden spoon to scrape up the sediment from the base of the pan. Pour over the onions and beef in the casserole.
6 Cover the casserole and cook in the oven for 1½ hours. Add the mixed vegetables and cook for a further 30 minutes or until the beef is tender when pierced with a sharp knife. Serve the stew hot, straight from the casserole.

Steak and parsnip pie

SERVES 4
750 g/1½ lb chuck steak, cut into bite-sized pieces
2 tablespoons vegetable oil
1 large onion, sliced
25 g/1 oz plain flour
400 g/14 oz can tomatoes
1 chicken stock cube
bouquet garni
salt and freshly ground black pepper
250 g/9 oz parsnips, cut into chunky pieces
215 g/7½ oz packet frozen puff pastry, defrosted
a little beaten egg, to glaze

1 Heat the oven to 180C/350F/Gas 4.
2 Heat the oil in a flameproof casserole, add the meat and onion and fry until the onion is soft and the meat is browned on all sides. Sprinkle in the flour, then cook for 1-2 minutes, stirring constantly.
3 Stir in the tomatoes and their juice, crumble in the stock cube and

Cook's Notes

TIME
Preparation time is 15 minutes. Cooking time is 2¾ hours but remember to allow time for the pastry to defrost.

●675 calories/2825 kj per portion

VARIATIONS
You could use blade or stewing steak, in which case the meat will need longer to cook. Turnips, carrots or swedes can be used instead of the parsnips or try using a mixture of root vegetables.

stir well to mix. Add the bouquet garni and season to taste with salt and pepper. Bring to the boil, stirring, then cover and transfer to the oven. Cook for 1½ hours or until the meat is just tender.
4 Stir in the parsnips and cook for a further 45 minutes.
5 Meanwhile, roll out the pastry on a floured surface to a shape slightly larger than the circumference of a 1 L/2 pint pie dish. Cut off a long narrow strip of pastry all around the edge. Reserve this and other trimmings.
6 Transfer the meat and parsnip mixture to the pie dish, then discard the bouquet garni and taste and adjust seasoning. Increase the oven

temperature to 220C/425F/Gas 7. Brush the rim of the pie dish with water, then press the narrow strip of pastry all around the rim. Brush the strip with a little more water, then place the large piece of pastry on top. Trim the edge of the pastry, then knock up and flute.
7 Make leaves or other shapes with the pastry trimmings, then place on top of the pie, brushing the underneath with water so that they do not come off during baking. Make a small hole in the centre of the pie for the steam to escape, then brush all over the pastry with beaten egg.
8 Bake the pie in the oven for 25-30 minutes until the pastry is well risen and golden brown. Serve hot.

Casseroled bacon

SERVES 4

1 kg/2 lb prime collar joint of bacon
  (see Buying guide)
1 tablespoon French mustard
1 tablespoon Demerara sugar
2 leeks, sliced
3 carrots, sliced
2 celery stalks, chopped
400 g/14 oz can tomatoes
1 teaspoon dried mixed herbs
freshly ground black pepper

1 Put the bacon in a large saucepan and cover with cold water. Bring to the boil, then lower the heat and simmer gently for 30 minutes (see Cook's tips).
2 Heat the oven to 180C/350F/Gas 4.
3 Drain the bacon and leave until cool enough to handle, then strip off the rind. Mix the mustard with sugar and spread over the fat surface.
4 Put the bacon in a large casserole and arrange the leeks, carrots and celery around it. Pour in the tomatoes with their juice, sprinkle in the herbs and add plenty of black pepper. Cover the casserole tightly (see Cook's tips) and cook in the oven for 45-60 minutes or until the juices run clear when the bacon is pierced with a skewer.
5 Serve the bacon carved into slices, with the vegetables and juices spooned over each portion.

TIME
Preparation and pre-boiling take about 45 minutes, cooking in the oven 45-60 minutes.

VARIATION
Use 2 large onions instead of leeks.

BUYING GUIDE
Collar, one of the less expensive bacon joints, is sold divided into end, middle and prime cuts. Prime is the best quality of these cuts.

COOK'S TIPS
There is no need to soak the bacon as the initial boiling removes the excess salt, but season the vegetables with pepper only.
  It is important to use a casserole with a really close-fitting lid, to prevent evaporation.

SERVING IDEAS
Serve with jacket-baked potatoes topped with soured cream and chives.

●565 calories/2375 kj per portion

Pork ragoût

SERVES 4

850 g/1¾ lb belly pork, trimmed of
  excess fat, cut into strips 2.5 cm/
  1 inch long and 2 cm/¾ inch wide
2 tablespoons vegetable oil
1 large onion, chopped
40 g/1½ oz plain flour
600 ml/1 pint chicken stock
4 large carrots, cut into thin slices
thinly pared zest of 1 lemon, cut
  into strips
100 g/4 oz black-eyed beans, soaked
  overnight in cold water, drained
½ teaspoon ground coriander
½ teaspoon ground turmeric
¼ teaspoon ground ginger
freshly ground black pepper
salt
strips of lemon zest and chopped
  parsley, to garnish

1 Heat the oven to 170C/325F/Gas 3.
2 Heat three-quarters of the oil in a flameproof casserole, add the pork and fry for 3-4 minutes until lightly browned and sealed on both sides. Remove with a slotted spoon and drain on absorbent paper.
3 Heat the remaining oil in the casserole, add the onion and fry gently for 5 minutes until soft and lightly coloured. Sprinkle in the flour and stir over low heat for 1-2 minutes. Gradually stir in stock. Bring to the boil and then simmer, stirring, until thick.
4 Add the carrots, lemon strips, beans and spices, and season to taste with ground black pepper. Bring back to the boil and then boil for 10 minutes. Return the meat to the casserole, cover and cook in the oven for about 2 hours.
5 Before serving, add salt and black pepper to taste, and garnish with the strips of lemon zest and the chopped parsley. Serve at once.

Kidney whirl

SERVES 4

500 g/1 lb lamb kidneys, skinned
2 tablespoons vegetable oil
2 shallots or 1 small onion, finely
   chopped
100 g/4 oz honey roast ham, roughly
   chopped
400 g/14 oz courgettes, sliced
1 tablespoon snipped chives
1 tablespoon lemon juice
salt and freshly ground black pepper
150 g/5 oz natural yoghurt
50 g/2 oz garlic and herb-flavoured
   soft cheese

TO GARNISH
1 lemon, sliced
snipped chives

1 Slice the kidneys in half and remove the cores with a small sharp knife or kitchen scissors.

2 Heat the oil in a deep flame-proof casserole, add the shallots and fry gently for about 5 minutes until softened. ☐ Add the kidneys and cook, stirring, for 5 minutes until they stiffen. Remove the kidneys with a slotted spoon and drain on absorbent paper.

3 Lower the heat, add the ham and courgettes to the pan and cook gently for 3-4 minutes. Add the chives, lemon juice and salt and pepper to taste and stir well. Place the kidneys on top, cover the casserole tightly and cook over gentle heat for about 30 minutes until the kidneys and courgettes are tender, stirring occasionally.

4 In a small bowl blend the yoghurt and cheese together until well-combined. Stir half into the kidney mixture, and heat through very gently without boiling, then remove from the heat and swirl in the remaining yoghurt mixture. Garnish with lemon slices and chives and serve at once, straight from the casserole.

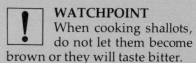

Liver in port

SERVES 4
500 g/1 lb lamb liver, cut into
   bite-sized pieces
25 g/1 oz plain flour
salt and freshly ground black pepper
2 teaspoons vegetable oil
15 g/½ oz margarine
1 small onion, finely chopped
100 g/4 oz button mushrooms,
   sliced
2 teaspoons French mustard
4 tablespoons hot chicken stock
2 tablespoons lemon juice
4 tablespoons port
1 teaspoon chopped fresh
   marjoram or ½ teaspoon dried
   marjoram
lemon slices, to garnish

1 Put the flour in a polythene bag and season with salt and pepper. Add the liver pieces and shake well to coat them thoroughly.
2 Heat the oil and margarine in a large frying-pan with a lid, add the onion and fry gently for 2 minutes. Add the liver pieces and fry quickly, stirring, to seal and brown.
3 Add the sliced mushrooms to the pan and cook for 1 further minute, stirring constantly.
4 In a small jug, blend the mustard with the stock, lemon juice and port and pour into the pan. Stir in the marjoram and season well with salt and pepper. Cover the pan and simmer gently for 10 minutes.
5 Transfer to a warmed serving dish, garnish with lemon slices and serve at once (see Serving ideas).

Cook's Notes

TIME
Preparation and cooking take only about 20 minutes.

SERVING IDEAS
Serve with creamed potatoes or a bowl of fluffy white rice, accompanied by a green vegetable such as French beans or broccoli.

●325 calories/1375 kj per portion

Turkey and ham salad

3 In a small bowl, mix together the mayonnaise, yoghurt and garlic, if using, and season with salt and pepper. Pour over the rice mixture and fold to mix again.

4 Gently stir the grapes and kiwifruit into the salad. Cover and keep in a cool place until required.

5 To serve: pile the salad on a bed of lettuce.

SERVES 4

175 g/6 oz cooked turkey, cut into
    bite-sized pieces
250 g/9 oz cooked ham, diced
250 g/9 oz long-grain rice
salt
1 small red pepper, deseeded and
    chopped
5 spring onions, chopped
4 tablespoons thick bottled
    mayonnaise
3 tablespoons natural yoghurt
1 clove garlic, crushed (optional)
freshly ground black pepper
100 g/4 oz grapes, halved, pips
    removed
3 ripe kiwifruit, peeled and sliced
    (see Buying guide and
    Preparation)
lettuce or chicory leaves, to serve

1 Cook the rice in plenty of boiling salted water for 12-15 minutes until tender, then rinse well under cold running water to separate the grains.

2 Put the drained rice into a large bowl, add the turkey, ham, pepper and spring onions and fold in gently.

Traditional roast chicken

SERVES 4

1.5 kg/3-3½ lb oven-ready chicken
25 g/1 oz butter, softened

STUFFING

100 g/4 oz fresh white breadcrumbs
50 g/2 oz shredded beef suet
2 tablespoons finely chopped fresh
    parsley
1 teaspoon dried mixed herbs
finely grated zest and juice of ½
    lemon
1 egg, beaten
salt and freshly ground black pepper

TO GARNISH

8 mini sausages or 4 chipolata
    sausages, twisted and halved
4 rashers streaky bacon, rinds
    removed, halved and rolled
    tightly
watercress sprigs

BREAD SAUCE

425 ml/¾ pint milk
1 onion, studded with 6 cloves
1 bay leaf
75 g/3 oz fresh white breadcrumbs
25 g/1 oz margarine or butter
pinch of freshly grated nutmeg

1 Heat the oven to 200C/400F/Gas 6.
2 Make the stuffing: put the breadcrumbs, suet, parsley, herbs and lemon zest in a bowl. Stir in the egg and lemon juice to bind and season to taste with salt and pepper.
3 Pat the chicken dry inside and out with absorbent paper. Stuff the neck end with the prepared stuffing, fold the neck skin over and secure with small skewers under the bird. Weigh the bird and calculate the cooking time at 20 minutes per 500 g/1 lb, plus 20 minutes.
4 Place the chicken in a roasting tin and spread it all over with butter. Cover with foil and roast in the centre of the oven until 40 minutes before the end of the calculated cooking time. Remove the foil and arrange the sausages and bacon rolls in the tin around the chicken, wedging the bacon rolls tightly between the sausages.
5 Return to the oven until the chicken, sausages and bacon rolls are golden brown and cooked through (the juices of the chicken run clear when the thickest part of the thigh is pierced with a skewer).
6 Meanwhile, make the bread sauce: pour the milk into a saucepan. Add the onion and bay leaf and heat gently to simmering point. Remove from heat, cover and leave for 30 minutes for the flavours to infuse.
7 Strain the milk, return to the saucepan, then add breadcrumbs and margarine. Season to taste with salt and pepper and heat slowly for about 10 minutes, stirring occasionally until thick and creamy. ⚠ Add the nutmeg, taste and season with more salt and pepper if necessary. Cover the surface of the sauce closely with cling film and keep hot.
8 Drain the chicken, sausages and bacon rolls well on absorbent paper. Place the chicken on a warmed serving dish and garnish with sausages, bacon rolls and watercress sprigs. Hand the bread sauce separately in a warmed sauceboat.

lower the heat and simmer gently for 30-40 minutes or until the peeled chestnuts are tender.

5 Meanwhile, bring a pan of salted water to the boil. Drain the sprouts and add to the pan. Cover and simmer for 8-10 minutes until just tender.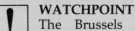

6 Drain the chestnuts and discard the celery. Drain the sprouts thoroughly, then return to the rinsed-out pan together with the chestnuts. Add the butter, nutmeg and salt and pepper to taste and toss to combine. Turn into a warmed serving dish and serve at once.

Cook's Notes

TIME
30 minutes preparation, plus 40-50 minutes cooking both the chestnuts and the sprouts.

COOK'S TIPS
The chestnuts must be kept hot to make peeling easier.
Ease last-minute preparations by preparing and cooking the chestnuts in advance.

! **WATCHPOINT**
The Brussels sprouts should be just tender but still firm; they will have a nice 'nutty' texture and flavour. If overcooked they will be soft and rather wet and will break up when combined with the chestnuts. Older, larger sprouts will take up to 20 minutes to cook.

BUYING GUIDE
If fresh chestnuts are not available, it is often possible to buy dried peeled chestnuts. Use 100 g/4 oz to each 500 g/1 lb sprouts. Place the dried chestnuts in a bowl, add boiling water to cover and leave to soak overnight. Drain and cook in the stock as in stage 4.

SERVING IDEAS
Serve with roast turkey or other roast poultry, or baked ham.

● 160 calories/675 kj per portion

Chestnut sprouts

SERVES 4
500 g/1 lb small Brussels sprouts
salt
250 g/9 oz chestnuts (see Buying guide)
150 ml/¼ pint chicken stock
1 celery stalk, halved
25 g/1 oz butter
pinch of freshly grated nutmeg
freshly ground black pepper

1 Wash the sprouts, cut off the stem ends and remove any discoloured leaves. Cut a cross in the stem end of each and leave to soak in a bowl of cold salted water.

2 Meanwhile, prepare the chestnuts: nick each with a sharp knife, then place in a saucepan and cover with cold water. Gradually bring to the boil and simmer for 10 minutes.

3 Remove the chestnuts from the heat, drain, then wrap in a thick folded tea-cloth to keep hot (see Cook's tips). Peel the chestnuts one at a time: hold in a soft cloth or oven glove, insert a small sharp knife into the slit in the skin and prise off the outer and inner skins.

4 Place the peeled chestnuts in a saucepan, cover with stock and add the celery. Bring to the boil, then

Turnip and potato clapshot

SERVES 4
350 g/12 oz small turnips, cut into chunks
500 g/1 lb potatoes, cut into chunks
salt
25 g/1 oz butter
freshly ground black pepper
2 tablespoons snipped chives

1 Bring the turnips to the boil in a large saucepan of salted water. Lower the heat and simmer for 5 minutes. Add the potatoes, return to the boil, then simmer for a further 10-15 minutes until the vegetables are tender.
2 Drain the vegetables well and mash to a fine purée. Beat in the butter, then season to taste with salt and pepper. Alternatively, put the drained potatoes and turnips with the butter and seasoning into the goblet of a blender and work until the mixture is completely smooth.
3 Turn the puréed vegetables into a warmed serving dish and sprinkle with the snipped chives. Serve at once (see Serving ideas).

Nutty apple pudding

SERVES 4

1 large cooking apple, weighing about 250 g/9 oz
juice of ½ lemon
40 g/1½ oz self-raising flour
pinch of salt
1 large egg
100 g/4 oz caster sugar
½ teaspoon vanilla flavouring
50 g/2 oz shelled walnuts, chopped
icing sugar, for dusting
butter or margarine, for greasing

1 Heat the oven to 180C/350F/Gas 4. Grease a 700 ml/1¼ pint soufflé or other ovenproof dish.

2 Quarter, peel, core and chop the apple. Sprinkle the pieces with lemon juice and turn gently.

3 Sift the flour and salt into a bowl and reserve.

4 Put the egg, sugar and vanilla into a large bowl and whisk together until thick and pale. Using a large metal spoon, gently fold in the sifted flour, then the apple and nuts.

5 Turn the mixture into the prepared dish and bake in the oven for 35-40 minutes, until well risen and browned around the edges. Sift icing sugar over the top and serve hot (see Serving ideas).

Cook's Notes

 TIME
The pudding takes just under 1 hour to prepare and bake in the oven.

 VARIATIONS
Sift ½ teaspoon ground cloves or cinnamon with the flour to spice up the flavour.
Use 2 firm pears in place of the apple and shelled pecans instead of the walnuts.

 SERVING IDEAS
This family pudding can be served as it is, or accompanied by custard, cream or vanilla ice cream.

●250 calories/1050 kj per portion

Sherry trifle

SERVES 4-6

**8 trifle sponges, cut in half
  horizontally**
100 g/4 oz raspberry jam
4 tablespoons medium sherry
**385 g/13½ oz can raspberries,
  drained with syrup reserved**
3 large eggs
2 tablespoons caster sugar
600 ml/1 pint milk
1 teaspoon vanilla flavouring
**300 ml/½ pint whipping or double
  cream**
red glacé cherries, halved
a little angelica, to finish

1 Spread the trifle sponges with the jam, then sandwich together again. Cut each across in half and arrange in the base of a glass serving bowl.
2 Stir the sherry into the reserved raspberry syrup, then pour over the sponges. Scatter the raspberries over the top.

3 Whisk the eggs and sugar lightly together in a large bowl (see Cook's tip). Heat the milk until almost boiling in a small saucepan, then pour on to the egg and sugar mixture, whisking constantly.
4 Strain the mixture into a heavy-based pan. [!] Cook over low heat for 10-15 minutes, [!] stirring constantly with a wooden spoon, until the custard is thick enough to coat the back of the spoon. Remove from the heat, stir in the vanilla and leave to cool for 10 minutes.
5 Pour the custard over the raspberries and sponges and leave to cool completely. Cover and refrigerate for 3-4 hours, or overnight.
6 Whip the cream until it forms soft peaks. Spread one-third of the cream over the custard and mark the surface with a fork or small palette knife, if liked. Put the remaining cream into a piping bag fitted with a large star nozzle. Pipe a border of cream and a lattice on the trifle, then decorate with cherries and angelica. Serve at once, or cover and refrigerate for 2-3 hours.

Mincemeat marzipan flan

SERVES 6

410 g/14½ oz jar mincemeat (see Buying guide)

215 g/7½ oz frozen shortcrust pastry, defrosted

grated zest of 1 small orange

1 small orange, segmented and coarsely chopped

1 dessert apple

25 g/1 oz fresh white breadcrumbs

75 g/3 oz almond marzipan (see Economy)

1 tablespoon icing sugar

1 Heat the oven to 200C/400F/Gas 6.

2 Roll out the pastry on a floured surface to a 25 cm/10 inch circle and use to line a 20 cm/8 inch loose-bottomed flan tin or ring, standing on a baking sheet. Trim off any excess pastry. Prick the base all over with a fork then refrigerate for 15 minutes.

3 Line the pastry case with greaseproof paper or foil and weight it down with baking beans. Bake in the oven for 20 minutes. Remove the greaseproof paper and beans.

4 Lower the oven temperature to 190C/375F/Gas 5. Return the flan case to the oven for a further 10 minutes, to completely dry out the pastry base.

5 Place the mincemeat in a bowl. Stir in the orange zest and segments. Peel, core and roughly chop the apple. Stir into the mincemeat with the breadcrumbs.

6 Roll out the marzipan on a surface lightly dusted with icing sugar, to a rectangle measuring 18 × 8 cm/7 × 3 inches. Cut the marzipan into 6 strips 18 cm/7 inches long and 1 cm/½ inch wide.

7 Spoon the mincemeat into the flan case. Place 3 marzipan strips, evenly spaced, across the flan and 3 the opposite way to form a lattice. Trim off any excess marzipan.

8 Bake in the oven for 15-20 minutes until the marzipan is just starting to melt and the filling is hot.

9 Allow the mincemeat marzipan flan to cool for 5 minutes then remove from the tin or ring. Serve the flan warm, or leave on a wire rack to cool completely.

Cook's Notes

TIME
Preparation 30 minutes, 15 minutes for chilling. Cooking time 50 minutes.

FREEZING
Cool completely then pack in a rigid container and seal, label and freeze for up to 3 months. To serve: defrost at room temperature for 2-3 hours. Serve cold or reheat in a 180C/350F/Gas 4 oven for 10-15 minutes and serve warm.

BUYING GUIDE
This sweet is an ideal way of using the less expensive ready-prepared brands of mincemeat that are currently available.

ECONOMY
Save any marzipan trimmings when making special cakes and use to make the lattice.

● 425 calories/1780 kj per portion

Festive ring

MAKES 12-15 SLICES
150 ml/¼ pint milk
2 large eggs, beaten
2 tablespoons water
500 g/1 lb strong white bread flour
1 teaspoon salt
1 teaspoon ground cinnamon
75 g/3 oz butter, diced
75 g/3 oz caster sugar
2 × 7 g/¼ oz sachets easy-blend
   dried yeast
175 g/6 oz seedless raisins
50 g/2 oz cut mixed peel
vegetable oil, for greasing

TO DECORATE
175 g/6 oz icing sugar
4-6 teaspoons lemon juice
100 g/4 oz almond marzipan
green food colouring

1 Heat the milk in pan until warm, then pour into a jug and beat in the eggs and water. Grease a large baking sheet with oil.

2 Sift the flour, salt and cinnamon into a warmed, large bowl, add the butter and rub in until the mixture resembles fine breadcrumbs. Stir in sugar, yeast, raisins and peel and mix well together.

3 Make a well in the centre of the dry ingredients, pour in the milk mixture and mix to a soft dough.

4 Turn the dough on to a lightly floured surface and knead for 10 minutes until elastic and smooth.

5 Cover the dough with lightly oiled polythene and leave to rise in a warm place for about 2 hours or until doubled in size.

6 Uncover the risen dough, punch down with knuckles, then knead lightly for about 2 minutes until the dough is smooth.

7 Using your hands, roll out on a lightly floured surface into a long, evenly-shaped roll, 60 cm/24 inches in length (approximately).

8 Coil dough round on the baking sheet to form into a ring, then dampen the ends and press firmly together. Cover with lightly oiled polythene and leave in a warm place for about 45 minutes or until almost doubled in size.

9 Heat the oven to 200C/400F/Gas 6.

Cook's Notes

TIME
30 minutes preparation, then 2¾ hours rising and 35 minutes baking. Allow cooling time, then 20 minutes for icing and 1 hour standing before decorating with the holly leaves and berries.

WATCHPOINT
Add the lemon juice a few drops at a time. If the icing is too thin it will run off bun ring altogether instead of dripping gradually.

● 385 calories/1600 kj per slice

10 Uncover the bun ring and bake in the centre of the oven for about 35 minutes until deep golden brown and cooked through. Transfer to a wire rack placed over a tray and leave until completely cold.

11 Blend the icing sugar with lemon juice to make a thick, smooth cream. ⚠ Spoon this over bun ring, allowing it to drip gradually down the sides. Leave ring on one side for approximately 1 hour to set.

12 Reserve a small piece of marzipan and colour remainder with green colouring, then roll out thinly on a board dusted with a little icing sugar and cut out into holly leaf shapes. Colour reserved marzipan red and roll into small balls to make holly berries.

13 Decorate the top of the iced bun ring with holly leaves and berries.

Christmas Dinner

This menu has been created to serve on that special festive occasion when traditional charm and flavour are appropriate. The meal begins with a melon and prawn cocktail that is suitably light and refreshing before the main course of stuffed turkey which is half boned to make carving easier. The pudding is flambéed as plum pudding should be, and served with brandy butter. So gather your friends and celebrate with our festive meal.

Melon and prawn cocktail

SERVES 8

1 small honeydew melon, deseeded and peeled
2 tablespoons red wine vinegar
4 tablespoons vegetable oil
1 teaspoon French mustard
1 tablespoon chopped fresh parsley
salt and freshly ground black pepper
1 large red dessert apple
3 celery stalks, thinly sliced
250 g/9 oz peeled prawns
8 unpeeled prawns, to garnish

1 Put the vinegar, oil, mustard and parsley into a bowl. Season with salt and pepper. Beat well.
2 Cut the melon into small neat cubes. Quarter and core the apple but do not peel it, then cut the flesh into neat cubes.
3 Put the melon, celery, apple and prawns into the dressing and mix lightly together. Spoon the melon and prawn mixture into 6 serving glasses. Garnish and serve at once.

Festive turkey

SERVES 8

4 kg/9 lb turkey, boned (see Buying guide and Preparation)
75 g/3 oz butter, softened
2 tablespoons plain flour
600 ml/1 pint turkey stock, made from the giblets and bones
sliced red and green pepper, to garnish

STUFFING

1 tablespoon corn oil
1 large onion, finely chopped
1 small red pepper, deseeded and chopped
1 small green pepper, deseeded and chopped
250 g/9 oz lean ham, chopped
175 g/6 oz fresh white breadcrumbs
2 teaspoons dried mixed herbs
3 tablespoons chopped fresh parsley
500 g/1 lb pork sausagemeat
1 egg
salt and freshly ground black pepper

---

1 Make the stuffing: heat the oil in a large frying-pan, add the onion and peppers and fry gently for 5 minutes until the onion is soft and lightly coloured. Cool completely.
2 Put the ham, breadcrumbs, herbs, sausagemeat and egg into a large bowl. Add the onion and peppers and season well with salt and pepper. Mix thoroughly together.
3 Heat the oven to 190C/375F/Gas 5.
4 Lay the boned turkey out flat on a board, skin-side down, and tuck in the small pieces of wing. Then trim off the excess skin at the neck and season the turkey well with salt and pepper. Stuff the body cavity and upper part of the legs where the bone has gone (to stop legs collapsing during roasting). Bring the sides of the turkey neatly up and over the stuffing to enclose it completely.
5 Using a large trussing needle and fine string, neatly sew up the turkey along the backbone where it was cut, to seal in the stuffing.
6 Turn the turkey over so that it is breast side up again. Press into a neat shape and tie the legs tightly together. Spread the skin with the softened butter and season with salt and pepper.
7 Wrap tightly in foil, put in roasting tin and roast for 2½ hours.
8 Remove the foil from the turkey and continue to roast for 60 minutes until the turkey is tender and the juices run clear when the thickest part of the thigh is pierced with a skewer.
9 Transfer the turkey to a warmed serving platter and allow to stand for at least 30 minutes to firm up before carving.
10 Meanwhile, make the gravy: drain off all the fat from the roasting tin, leaving behind the turkey juices. Sprinkle in the flour and cook over low heat until lightly coloured. Stir in the stock and bring to the boil, scraping up all the sediment from the base of the tin. Reduce the heat slightly and simmer gently for 10-15 minutes. Strain into a warmed sauceboat.
11 Just before serving, remove the string from the turkey and garnish with red and green pepper slices. To serve, carve into slices, cutting right across the bird. Remove the legs in the normal way.

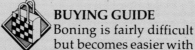

Plum pudding

MAKES 2 × 1 L/1¾ PINT PUDDINGS
225 g/8 oz stoned prunes, roughly
    chopped
225 g/8 oz seedless raisins
100 g/4 oz dried apricots, roughly
    chopped
100 g/4 oz sultanas
100 g/4 oz glacé cherries, roughly
    chopped
50 g/2 oz cut mixed peel
finely grated zest and juice of
    1 orange
finely grated zest and juice of
    1 lemon
1 teaspoon ground mixed spice
4 tablespoons dark rum or brandy
175 g/6 oz butter
100 g/4 oz soft dark brown sugar
50 g/2 oz black treacle
3 large eggs
225 g/8 oz fresh breadcrumbs
100 g/4 oz ground almonds
2-3 tablespoons dark rum or
    brandy, to flame
margarine, for greasing

1 Put all the dried fruit in a large mixing bowl with the orange and lemon zest and juice, spice and rum. Mix well, then cover and leave for 1 hour, stirring occasionally.
2 Cut rounds of greaseproof paper to fit the bases of two 1 L/1¾ pint pudding basins, then cut 2 more rounds to fit the tops of the basins.
3 Thoroughly grease the 2 pudding basins, then line the bases with the rounds of paper. Grease the paper.
4 Beat the butter, sugar and treacle together in a large mixing bowl until pale and fluffy. Add the eggs one at a time, beating after each addition.
5 Add the breadcrumbs and ground almonds to butter mixture and mix very well. Add the soaked fruit with all of the juices and mix thoroughly. Cover and leave to stand for 30 minutes.
6 Divide the pudding mixture between prepared basins and level each surface. Grease one side of the remaining greaseproof paper rounds, then place, greased side down, on top of each basin. Cover each basin with greased and pleated foil and secure with fine string.
7 Stand each basin in a large heavy-

based saucepan and pour in enough boiling water to come half-way up sides of the basin. Cover with well-fitting lid and simmer for 8 hours.
8 Protecting your hands with oven gloves, lift the puddings out of the pans and remove the foil. Cover with clean tea-towels and allow to cool. When cold, re-cover with clean foil and store puddings in a cool dry airy place (see Cook's tip).
9 To serve: reheat for 2-3 hours as in stage 7. Lift puddings out of pans and remove foil and greaseproof paper coverings. Turn on to a warmed serving platter and remove greaseproof paper linings.
10 To flame puddings: put the rum into a cup, then stand the cup in hot water to warm the spirit. Pour the spirit over the pudding and set alight. Take to the table at once, while still alight, and serve as soon as all the flames have died down.

Brandy butter

SERVES 6-8
75 g/3 oz unsalted butter, softened
150 g/5 oz icing sugar, sifted
1-2 tablespoons brandy
1 egg white (optional – see
    Cook's tip)

1 In a large bowl, beat the butter with a wooden spoon until creamy.
2 Beat in the sugar until it is well mixed and thick and smooth, then beat in brandy to taste.
3 Whisk egg white, if using, until stiff, then fold into brandy butter.
4 Transfer the butter to a serving bowl, rough up the surface with a fork, then chill in the refrigerator for at least 2 hours before serving.

Plum Pudding

TIME
45 minutes preparation, plus 1½ hours standing time, 8 hours cooking, plus 2-3 hours reheating.

COOK'S TIP
The puddings will keep, stored in a cool dry airy cupboard, for 2-3 months. However, unlike most rich fruit puddings, they can be eaten 1-2 days after making.

PRESSURE COOKING
Cook the puddings one at a time. Pour 1.5 L/2½ pints water into the cooker and add a few drops of lemon juice. Place a trivet, rim side down, in the cooker. Stand the pudding basin on trivet. Steam without pressure for 30 minutes, then bring to high (H) pressure and cook for 3 hours. Reduce pressure slowly.

SERVING IDEAS
Each pudding serves 6-8 people. Serve the pudding with brandy butter (see recipe) or whipped cream.

●440 calories/1850 kj per portion

Brandy Butter

TIME
Preparation takes about 15 minutes. Allow at least 2 hours for chilling the brandy butter before serving.

COOK'S TIP
Adding an egg white gives a lighter texture.

VARIATIONS
For *almond brandy butter*, replace 50 g/2 oz of the sugar with the same weight of ground almonds.

For *citrus brandy butter*, add the grated zest of an orange or lemon, with juice to taste.

For *rum butter*, use dark rum in place of brandy and brown sugar instead of icing sugar.

For *sherry butter*, use medium sherry and caster sugar.

For *whisky butter*, use whisky and soft brown sugar.

●200 calories/850 kj per portion

Index

Picture Credits

S. & O. Matthews 30/31
E.M. Megson 78/79
Harry Smith 6/7, 54/55
All other pictures from
Marshall Cavendish Picture Library.